Danielle,

There is no waste in waiting for God's perfect plan. Everything is beautiful in its season

*signature*
30/07/2017

# Wholeness in Singleness

## WISDOM FOR WIVES IN WAITING

Brittney Jones

Wholeness in Singleness: Wisdom for Wives in Waiting

Copyright © 2017 by Brittney Jones

All Rights Reserved. No part of this publication may be reproduced or used in any manner whatsoever without the prior written permission of the publisher except for the use of brief quotations in a book review.

ISBN-13: 978-1540485700

ISBN-10: 1540485706

# *Table of Contents*

Foreword .................................................................................. i

Introduction ............................................................................ ii

1. The Blessing of Being Single ............................................. 1
2. Deception of the Media .................................................... 7
3. Stereotypes and Standards .............................................. 13
4. Who Is in Your Circle? .................................................... 18
5. What Is Love? ................................................................. 25
6. A Matter of Trust ............................................................ 34
7. Is It Well with Your Entire Well-Being? ........................ 40
8. The Purpose of Marriage ................................................ 47
9. Grown Woman Dealing with Her Little Girl ................ 52
   - Self-Image ................................................................... 53
   - Passion ........................................................................ 56
   - Rejection ..................................................................... 58
10. Daddy Issues ................................................................... 67
11. Soul Ties ......................................................................... 74
12. Lonely but Not Alone .................................................... 82
13. The Anguish of Anger .................................................... 86
14. The Struggle of Strongholds .......................................... 91
    - Impulsive Spending .................................................... 93
    - Food ............................................................................ 93
    - Relationships ............................................................. 94
    - Work ........................................................................... 95
    - Self .............................................................................. 96
    - Pornography .............................................................. 98

15. The Angst of Abuse ................................................... 103
16. Know Your Value ..................................................... 114
17. Guarding Your Heart ................................................ 118
18. Draw the Line, and Don't Cross It ............................ 124
19. A Stand for Purity .................................................... 131
20. "That Guy" ............................................................... 138
21. Mission of Maturity ................................................. 142
22. Wife Material .......................................................... 149
    - Effective Communicator ................................... 150
    - Prayer Warrior .................................................. 151
    - Gifted Servant .................................................. 153
    - Submissive ....................................................... 154
    - Stewardship ..................................................... 155
23. A Woman with Goals .............................................. 158
24. Virtuous Woman ..................................................... 163
25. What's the Motive? .................................................. 170
26. Red Flags ................................................................ 176
27. Hold Out for Your Husband ................................... 187
28. Bonus ...................................................................... 191

To my loving parents, Ronald and Peatra Jones,

thank you for your unwavering support and encouragement.

# *Foreword*

The author, Brittney Jones, has produced, by the wisdom of the Holy Spirit, a literary work that will save generations of singles from much grief. The content is wisdom beyond her years. She makes no concessions about the fact that singleness is a blessing and wholeness is a necessity. It is not a curse to be single.

This book will answer a multitude of common questions that singles have and correct a myriad of false ideas people believe about marriage. She exposes the roots of some twisted concepts that distort reality and interrupt the happiness of singles. She lays out a laundry list of necessary objectives every single should attend to, to maximize her potential while waiting.

This book is a fast ride to inner healing and divine perspective. It will cause the reader to understand their pain and where it comes from. She deals with matters like: "daddy issues", soul ties and strongholds. I also love the fact that she brings into account the personal responsibility of choosing one's circle well to develop your best life.

Brittney ultimately brings the reader to a full biblical understanding of what a wife is and what it takes to be one. She makes it clear that it is unacceptable to settle for anything short of a real husband. When you're done reading this book you will find great peace in waiting. You will also find a deeper wisdom in the process.

**R.C. Blakes, Jr.**

## Introduction

"To everything there is a season, and a time to every purpose under the heaven" Ecclesiastes 3:1 (NIV). Everything in life operates in seasons and being single is no different. Our society sees the season of singleness as a curse instead of the blessing that it is. A lot of pressure is placed on single young women to get to the *destination* of marriage, and many bypass the season of preparation during singleness. Driven by the fear of being alone, biological clocks running out of time, and seeing other friends get engaged and married, many young women find themselves being unprepared for marriage or in premature relationships.

Some single women idolize marriage and think of it as the solution to all their problems. They think, "I will finally be happy when I get a husband." But that mindset will leave us disappointed because the institution of marriage was never meant to be worshiped. It is merely a reflection of our relationship with God that is to be enjoyed for His glory. Therefore, it is important to have the right view of God and of the marital relationship that He created. We must also have the right view of our desires, so that the pursuit of those desires does not take precedence over God. When we firstly seek the Lord and His kingdom, everything else—including marriage—will be added if it is in His will.

Singleness is the season to become your best self so that you can be a helpmeet to your husband as you both fulfill God's design for marriage. The journey to wholeness is like a season of reconstruction. It requires you to destroy ungodly soul ties and break strongholds. You will need to establish a standard of holiness and set healthy boundaries. Seek fellowship and encouragement from other believers, and detach yourself from the negative influences of society. Renew your mind and develop spiritual discernment. Now is the time to take back your power from the past and give a voice to your unspoken truths. Become the woman that God has created you to be and walk in your purpose. Develop good virtues, progress in your faith, and find your identity and value in Christ. That is what it means to be whole.

As you seek after the things of Christ, you will become His image bearer. Your relationship with Him will be reflected in your relationship with yourself and with others. As you pursue holiness, you will find wholeness because your relationship with the Lord is the source of everything else in your life. That is the primary focus of this book—to point you back to God and allow Him to prepare you during your singleness for the season of marriage. Although you may not be able to prepare for everything that marriage will bring, your foundation in Christ will be everything that you need to flourish.

Many of us face challenges with self-worth, rejection, fatherlessness, anger, abuse, addictions, sexual impurity, and loneliness among numerous other struggles. But as wives in waiting, we have the power to overcome these challenges through Christ. He wants to turn our messes into masterpieces for His glory. He wants to work in us and through us so that someday we can be presented to our future husbands as helpmeets.

In this book, you will find wisdom and practical ways to fully prepare yourself for your future husband. This is not a playbook on how to get a man in a month. This is also not a checklist of things to do to manipulate the hand of God so that you can get married. This is about checking the motives of your heart, beginning the process of healing from past issues, and maximizing your single season for the glory of God as you wait on His perfect timing. I will share the lessons I have learned during my own journey, as well as journal entries that I have written during my season of singleness. Each chapter will begin with a scripture and end with a prayer. Join me on the journey to finding wholeness in singleness.

# CHAPTER ONE

## *The Blessing of Being Single*

"Every good and perfect gift is from above, coming down from the Father of the heavenly lights, who does not change like shifting shadows." James 1:17 (NIV)

Have you ever realized how crazed society is about relationships and marriage? The topic dominates coffee shops and dinner tables as we grow more and more obsessed with which celebrities have broken up or which friend just started dating. We've placed so much urgency on being in a relationship that the very idea of being single is enough to crush the spirit, cripple the mind, and rob the single woman's heart of its joy. Many women have become so preoccupied with pursuing mere men while bypassing the Creator of all men. They become so busy running after relationships or lamenting the lack thereof, that they run past the blessing in being single. Compounded by the pressure of friends, jeers of coworkers, and teasing of family members, a high-speed chase after a man soon ensues. In desperation, some women pursue any man with a pulse, regardless of whether he has an active relationship with God, attainable personal goals, Godly morals, or simply a legal job. As a result of pursuing instead of being pursued, these women compromise their value just to avoid feeling lonely and incomplete. Many broken relationships today were built on flimsy societal expectations that are destined to crumble.

And then there are the women who may not directly pursue a man but are disgruntled with waiting. She allows her untamed emotions to take flight on the wings of vain imaginations. Her mind drifts with thoughts about whether the new coworker or the man across the room could possibly be her future husband. She begins to entertain thoughts of infatuation that turn into fantasies of marriage and children. Before she knows it, she has fallen in love with the sound of her first name followed by his last name—and it's all in her head!

Our minds have become so engrossed with the pursuit of romantic love. But the truth is, we don't know what genuine love is! Rather, we are in love with the idea of being "in love." We are obsessed with the idea of being someone's significant other, holding hands, taking long walks, and sharing candle-lit dinners. This is the way the media has depicted the stereotypical relationship. We admire the exterior of a fantasy without knowing the truth of the reality. There is so much more to marriage than romantic dinners and enchanted movie dates. Those perks should merely be the icing of the cake.

Whether you are the desperate or the disgruntled single woman, you have a choice to make. You can either choose to wait on the Lord and allow Him to prepare you, or prematurely jump into a relationship that He did not ordain. Of course, the latter comes with consequences when we are driven by the wrong motives, desperation, or distrust in God's timing.

At the doorstep of compromise, many women are knocking and hoping that *happily ever after* will open the door. They are greeted by shear disappointment in the form of a man who does not respect or recognize their value. Some women still choose to enter a *house* of abuse, unhappiness, loneliness, and broken-heartedness because they have settled into relationships outside of the will of God. Sometimes those of us who are strong enough to pick up the pieces and keep moving, go from house to house, knocking on the doors of the hearts of men—doors that God never intended to be opened to us.

So many women have wasted their time by engaging in years of dead-end relationships because their feelings overpowered their faith in God. They continue to kiss 'frogs' hoping for one of them to turn into Prince Charming. But you can't put a crown on a 'Joker' and expect him to behave like a 'King.' That means you must first recognize that you are a valuable Queen—created in the image of God with inherent dignity and worth.

In the palace of our minds, we sometimes get caught up in fulfilling shallow societal standards, that leave us feeling discouraged and empty. Questions like "Will I ever get married?" and "How much longer do I have to wait?" plague our minds. But what if we aren't asking the right questions? Instead, what if we shifted the relationship paradigm to ask "Am I preparing for what I prayed for?" or "Am I embodying the qualities that I desire in a husband?" What if we focus more on our readiness to serve and be submissive? What if we face our fears, bring closure to past issues, and walk in our purpose? Are we truly ready for God to strip our hearts of its desire to want a husband more than it wants Him? Are we truly ready to be renewed with a mindset that first finds contentment in God? Are we ready to give up our weak attempts to fill our voids and allow God to satisfy them? If not, we aren't ready for marriage.

Until we find wholeness in Christ we will find ourselves disappointed by temporary bliss that ultimately blisters our hearts. There is no relationship that will ever be able to complete us the way that God can. That is the blessing of being single! Find completion and contentment in the Lord while trusting Him to honor the desire of your heart to be married. Allow Him to strip you of the negative societal influences, and remind you of the assurance of His love and perfect plan for your life. Discover your identity in Christ and walk in His purpose for your life. Sit at His feet and spend uninterrupted time with Him. Allow Him to heal your heart and your brokenness.

The beauty of being single is sabotaged when we try to abide by society's ever-changing 'relationship rules' which are based on superficial standards for single women. They once dictated that a woman should graduate high school by eighteen, graduate college by twenty-two, start a career by twenty-four, get married by twenty-six, and start a family by thirty. However, this ideal is changing as culture begins to normalize premarital sex and cohabitation, and marriage is seemingly becoming optional.

Too many women have created their own plans and tried to box God into them. Sometimes we get paranoid as we perceive that time is ticking away. The biological clock says that it will be too risky to have a baby after the age of thirty-five. The societal clock says dating will be difficult after the age of thirty. The physical clock says we are not going to have flawless skin and hair and for the rest of our lives. But when will we stop looking at these clocks and realize that God does not operate on our time? Chasing relationships God didn't ordain, comparing ourselves to others, and throwing disgruntled pity parties only diminishes the valuable time that can be spent becoming whole and fulfilling God's purpose for our lives.

There is not a checklist of things to do by a specific time before God presents you to your future husband. However, there is a blessing in preparing for marriage. Maximize this time by discovering who you are, why you are here, and how God will use you and your experiences for His glory. That is the blessing of being single.

## Prayer

Dear God, society is crazed about relationships and the pressures are too heavy to bear. Please free me from societal expectations and help me to wait on You. I want to see singleness as the blessing that You have created it to be. Please help me to find my value and purpose in You. Lord, I choose to believe that Your plan for my life is perfect and that at the right time, You will present me to my future husband. Help me use my season of singleness to draw nearer to You, not only in preparation for becoming a wife but to seek to advance your kingdom here on earth. Amen.

# CHAPTER TWO

## *Deception of the Media*

"Jesus answered: 'Watch out that no one deceives you.'" Matthew 24:4 (NIV)

From the time we were little girls, some of us have been conditioned by fairy tales like *The Princess and the Frog, Beauty and the Beast, and Cinderella* that painted a picture of what our lives and love stories should be like. These fairytales have conditioned the minds of little girls to associate happiness and fulfillment in life, with their relationship status, their popularity, and acceptance. Magical love stories even made their way into our childhood playtime sessions. Our perceptions of love have innocently been shaped by the fantasies of Barbie and Ken riding off into the sunset in a pink Volkswagen. And now as adults, many of us hope to make those fantasies a reality. So many women place themselves in the 'glass slippers' of their favorite character, hoping to be romanced into a fairytale ending.

## Deception of the Media

In today's romance movies, love has been confused with sex. Sex has become a marketing tool that the media uses to make millions of dollars in profit. Media also contributes to the over-sexualizing of society to the point that it is virtually impossible to watch a television show or movie without a couple of intense sex scenes. It should be alarming to us when an erotic movie like *Fifty Shades of Grey* profits over $500 million dollars in the worldwide box office. Even some music videos that sexually objectify women get millions of hits upon release. This suggests that society has an appetite for sensual material, even at the expense of degrading the bodies of women. Many media companies benefit from this craving for lust—a craving that can never be completely satisfied. This is the reason we find ourselves consuming a massive amount of time on television, music videos, and social media without ever being completely fulfilled.

The influence of media has now become more pervasive and prevalent than ever before. At the tap of a button, we have access to the posts, photos, and blogs of social media. These media platforms sow seeds in our hearts and minds, which in turn affect our behaviors, thoughts, and feelings. We lose ourselves trying to find acceptance at the expense of authenticity. Social media has become a stage for the embellished exhilarations and exaggerated experiences posted online. We measure our value by the number of likes, retweets, views, and followers that are gained. As soon as a photo or status update is posted, we sit in anxious anticipation of notifications for an update. From breakfast to bedtime, photos that are overloaded with hashtags are posted in the hope of attracting more attention.

Social media has also made us selfish and hungry for popularity. Even some celebrities and public figures do just about anything to gain more media time. We see them scantily dressed, releasing sex tapes, and posing naked for magazines. The deception is that the more we overshare the filtered and fabricated parts of our lives, the more valuable and likeable we become. We seek to be "liked" but what we need is to be loved.

Speaking of love, every day on my timeline I see someone gets engaged, married, or starts a new relationship. A huge part of me is genuinely happy for other people's companionship, but a small part of me still wonders when it will be my turn. You may have the same thoughts from time to time and that's okay. But having our thoughts turn into an obsession is unhealthy and in many cases, leads to discouragement or even idolatry. The unhealthy glorification of relationships has made some of us envious of other couples because we also want to feel loved. But if we are not careful, feelings of envy, despair, and insecurity can creep into our hearts and lead us to pursue premature relationships.

Media content should not be the benchmark for comparisons or assessments of our value. People are not always what they *post* to be. Even reality television isn't real—it is scripted "entertainment." Behind closed doors, the couple on SnapChat may not be happy. Behind closed doors, the relationship on Facebook may not have been God-ordained. Oops! Someone had to tell you the truth. People only show us an edited snapshot of their lives. We don't know how many of those persons still secretly experience an overwhelming lack of true love. We do not see the many sleepless nights, arguments, and other issues that happen when the cameras stop rolling. So how can we become covetous of people who have the same struggles and need for love that we do?

There is more to life than unfulfilling relationships, popularity and acceptance that the media does not show us. The relationships that you see are not as perfect as they appear. The party that you missed was not as exciting as it seemed. The outfit that you are envious of may have been borrowed. The car you are jealous of may have been rented. If we are not careful with our media consumption and the seeds sown in our hearts, we can be drawn away from reality—the reality that we need a love that can never be found in "likes" and follows.

We were all created with the need to love and to be loved. The ways that we try to meet the need for love can either completely satisfy us or leave us longing for more. The media tells us that if we are successful, wealthy, popular, or powerful, we would experience love and happiness. These things may draw attention to ourselves, but not our true and authentic selves. People are impressed by our strengths but they identify with our weaknesses. We don't have to be perfect to inspire, encourage, or be "liked" by others. We can inspire others in our state of imperfection because it places the glory of God on display.

Our usage and consumption of the media should be a platform that in some way points others back to God. We should use it to positively influence other young single women and remind them that although the temptations may be great, God is greater. Remind them that their value is not found in wealth or popularity but in

Christ. Remind them that they don't need to be 'liked' by others when Christ has loved them.

God pursues us with His love—the type of love that completely satisfies. When we accept the love that He freely gives, we don't have to seek the attention and approval of others to affirm our value. As God continues to pour out His love toward us, we in turn can share it with others through our online and offline interactions. It is then that we can be our true selves and share the ways that God is working in our lives—the content that is posted and the content that never becomes public knowledge. These personal interactions stimulate authenticity as we talk about the parts of our lives that we will never share via social media. That is the way to bring us back to the reality that is often lost in the fantasies of the media.

It is important for us to remember that media can be misused as a platform for people to misrepresent themselves in the way they want to be perceived by the world. If we buy into the deception of the media, it will leave us feeling empty, broken, and confused. Our lives may never match their filtered and photo-shopped fallacies. The Bible says that we should see to it that no one misleads us. The only way to not be misled is to know the truth found in God's Word. Here is the truth—you are greatly loved by God who pursues you continuously. Your value in His eyes is not contingent on how popular you are on social media. Once you understand the depth of His infinite love for you, you will no longer be deceived by the media.

## **Prayer**

Jesus, You are the standard that I pattern my life after. Help me to live for an audience of One and not to be inappropriately influenced by the media. Help me to be content with my reality and not center my life on fantasies, falsified images, videos, blogs, and statuses. I do not want to be jealous or envious of the relationships of others. I'd rather celebrate with them, knowing that You can bring that same joy to my life in due season. Open my eyes that I may not be deceived by the standards of the world's system. Amen.

# CHAPTER THREE

## *Stereotypes and Standards*

"Stop judging by mere appearances, but instead judge correctly."
John 7:24 (NIV)

If you have been single for any amount of time, you have probably encountered numerous inquisitive minds that want to know why you are not in a relationship. The questions that people ask are mostly framed in the context of "what is wrong with you?" They start to pass judgements based on stereotypes to explain your singleness as if it were a disease. In fact, your personal life is of such keen interest to them that they start to rationalize your singleness. Maybe you are too busy, too assertive, or too stuck up. Maybe you are still heartbroken. Maybe you are too career-driven and intelligent. Maybe your standards are too high. The list of these stereotypical explanations for your singleness is exhaustive. But why must there be something wrong with you choosing to be single? What if we reframed the context of its questions to ask "What is right with you?" Maybe then we would begin to understand that there is nothing wrong with being young, whole, single, and virtuous—simultaneously. Maybe we would realize that coming across a single woman with standards may seem rare, but it is not wrong.

If you find yourself being ridiculed for having high standards and misunderstood for choosing to remain single until God changes your status, then you are in a good place! It means that you have not conformed to the societal pressure to be in transient relationships. It means that you can serve as a beacon of light that displays the blessing in being single. It means that you can defy societal stereotypes because there is nothing wrong with being content during a period of singleness.

Now I must admit that it is sometimes awkward and I dare say annoying, when people repeatedly question you about when will you 'find' a man, or make jokes about you being an old lady with twelve cats. Some may tell you that it is too difficult to live holy in an unholy world. Others may tell you that singleness is the time to sleep around to gain sexual experience, live loosely, and have fun before finally settling down. But counter to their criticism is the truth of your conviction—the conviction that God's timing is perfect and until He reveals you to your husband, you will remain holy. In fact, the same people who jeer at you are probably jealous because they didn't uphold the standards that you have for themselves. They will try to tell you that living wildly is 'rewarding' but will never share their regrets. My sister, I urge you to stand firmly on your convictions and do not conform to this world's standards.

As a confident woman, you must choose to live outside of the box of stereotypes. When you know who you are and what you desire, you will exude the boldness and courage to defy stereotypes, break out of boxes, and live up to God's standard alone. I understand the difficulty of not crumbling under the judgments of others, especially when it is so much easier to fit in than to stand out. But whenever the voices of others take precedence over the voice of God, you will find yourself in 'people bondage.' Too often we look to the world and not the Word for our standard of living. We are afraid of what friends would think or say if we dared to live outside of their expectations. But the more we try to please people, the more we lose our sense of self. Learn to live for the approval of God and not the acceptance of people. Then the *sting* of stereotypes by those who do not know the standard God has asked you to uphold, will be less potent. Don't allow anyone to make you feel sorry for being single.

There is nothing wrong with you or the season that you are now in. You are not missing anything because you are exactly where God needs you to be at this time. Your relationship status does not determine your worth. Don't become so focused on the future that you miss the blessing of the present. Instead of conforming to societal stereotypes and expectations, set a higher standard. Soon those who ridiculed you will begin to respect you and most importantly, respect the God in you. Pray that those who jeered at your singleness will join you on a journey to wholeness.

Having this kind of influence on others requires you to be consistent in your standards both in private and in public—in both your Facebook statuses and your direct messages. Keep God in the biography section of your Instagram but also in every section of your daily life. That is the test of character—doing and saying the right thing even when no one is looking. Always remember that people will hear what you say but they also watch what you do. And to inspire them, there must be consistency between the two.

Standards are not just rules that you live by. They are not legalistic guidelines of things to do and not do. But it is seeing yourself the way that God sees you, and deporting yourself in a manner that is reflective of the worth He places on your life. Know that you are valuable. Treat your body with respect and take care of yourself. Remain true to your morals and maintain a positive perspective.

The world has wrongfully formulated so many stereotypes about single women. It expects you to be miserable because you are lonely, to be a wild partier because you don't have a partner, or to be a workaholic because you have no other life. The world expects you to operate in insecurity and to be attention-seeking. It expects you to be desperate and clingy, or hateful and resentful toward men. But as a Godly single woman, none of these stereotypes should characterize you. In your striving to be more like Christ, it is inevitable that you will become an anomaly. Always keep in mind that if you live for the approval of others, then you are not a servant of Christ (Galatians 1:10).

Living for the approval of God automatically elevates your standards and places you outside of the societal box. That is where you belong! The next time someone bombards you with questions about being single, simply tell them that your singleness is a choice. A choice to not settle. A choice to not allow your value to be determined by your relationship status. A choice to be happy and to maximize this period of your life. It is a choice to not compromise your standards or submit to their stereotypes.

## Prayer

Lord, I choose to live outside of the box and not to succumb to the stereotypes and expectations of society as a single woman. Help me to only seek Your approval and please give me the courage to live holy in an unholy world. Help me to be consistent in upholding my standards so that I can be an inspiration to other single women. Lord, I want to exemplify what it means to not conform to the standards of this world so that my life may point others back to You. Amen.

# CHAPTER FOUR

## *Who Is in Your Circle?*

"Walk with the wise and become wise, for a companion of fools suffers harm." Proverbs 13:20 (NIV)

The older you get, the more you will realize how much your circle of friends changes. At least that is the story of my life. Some friends teach you a lesson before leaving, others walk with you for a season, and others still are there to love you for a lifetime. As you continue to grow, you learn who is a part of your history and who will be a part of your destiny. Maybe you are still close with someone from the second grade or met your best friend in college. Maybe you lost a friend when you moved to another location or grew apart from someone when you entered a new stage of life. Maybe you fell out of touch with a friend because your interests changed or you gained a friend because you found a new hobby. As people and situations change, so will your circle of friends and the nature of each friendship. We are ever-evolving and therefore our friendships likewise undergo changes.

I like to visualize friendships like the circles on a dartboard. The circles vary in size and get smaller as they approach the bull's eye—you! The very outer circle is acquaintances—people you do not see often and who maybe know a fact or two about you, but have no consistent and deep connection with you. Those in the middle circle are casual friends who may share common interests with you, know surface-level information about your life, and may encourage you along the way but there are no deep emotional attachments. Finally, your inner circle of friends consists of people who have seen you at your high and low points of life. You probably speak with them on a frequent basis and your conversations get into the intimate details of your life. These are the people you completely trust with the treasure of you heart.

Inner circle friends may be few but great in value because of a mutual commitment to see each other thrive in every area of life. They are loyal, respectful, understanding, supportive, trustworthy, and dependable. They are good listeners, give sound advice, and correct you in love. The closer the circle is to you, the greater the level of intimacy, responsibility, and accountability.

A great way for you to gain close friends is by being in community with others with whom you share similar values, interests, and beliefs. A community is central to building social capital where networks of friends offer prayer, Godly counsel, and correction. They reveal new ways to challenge yourself and affirm your strengths while helping to strengthen your weak areas. A healthy community creates an atmosphere for growth in the things of Christ, provides opportunities to serve others, and creates an atmosphere of transparency and authenticity. There are allowances for the confession of sins and the receiving of support through personal struggles.

The journey of life and indeed this season of being single becomes a little easier when you are in community with others. Community helps to keep you grounded in your morals, encourages you to stay focused on your goals, teaches life lessons, and walks with you through both delightful and difficult days.

Maybe you have been praying for God to send you some friends who would be this kind of a blessing in your life. That is a great prayer to pray and I believe that God can connect you to these types of people. It is also imperative that your desire for friendship be accompanied by discernment. The first 'nice' person that you meet after that prayer, may not necessarily be the answer to that prayer. Be careful to not intimately connect yourself with just anyone that you come across. Discern the people who walk into your life spiritually, before becoming connected to them physically.

Some friendships are based on convenience, others are distractions, and others still are assignments from the Enemy to pull you away from your purpose. Some friendships start healthy and later become toxic. People change and seasons change and you should be sensitive to those changes. Not all friendships will last forever, so do not be afraid to let go of your seasonal friends once they have served their purpose in your life. The longer you cling to them, the unhealthier the friendship will become. <u>Don't give seasonal friends lifetime privileges.</u>

Genuine friendships happen organically, and you won't have to force the conversations and interactions. Friendships should be purposeful and pure. They should never be built on fear, manipulation, lies, over-dependency, possessiveness, jealousy, distrust, abuse, or control. Godly friends bring out the best in you and are intentional about making positive investments in your life.

Since the characteristics of your friends become a part of your character, be certain that the mannerisms and habits you pick up from the people closest to you are positive. First Corinthians 15:33 tells us that "…bad company corrupts good character." Make sure that the influence that your friends have on your life builds you up and doesn't pull you down. If your close friendships ever cease to be mutually fruitful and stop growing in the things of Christ, they have the potential to become toxic. At that point you should prayerfully proceed in either making improvements to remain healthily connected, or decide to sever the ties.

Choose friends who will encourage you to stay close to the Lord. They should be encouraging you in the things that are right, pure, lovely, and praiseworthy. Your friends should sow seeds of encouragement and remind you to rely on God to be your source of hope, joy, peace of mind, and contentment. These types of friends become blessings, not burdens to be around. They pour wisdom into your life and encourage you to trust the Lord with His plan for every area of your life. Any friendship that doesn't push you toward God needs to be carefully evaluated and possibly terminated. That is not to say that you cannot be friends with unbelievers, because they too need to see the light of Christ through you. However, be careful to be a positive influence while not compromising your integrity.

I am grateful for a small circle of friends who are not afraid to keep it real with me and ask the difficult questions. They tell me when I am wrong, help me calm down when I am stressed, and listen to my concerns. My friends are like rearview and side mirrors—they show me my blind spots and help to bring me back on the right path. When I believe I 'know it all,' they turn on a few more light bulbs in my head. My inner circle holds me accountable to my standards and never asks me to compromise on them. They offer encouragement and pray for and with me.

Girls' nights out and *girlie* chit chats are some of my most cherished and appreciated memories—times when I have had the opportunity to lay my heart out on the table and be completely honest with my friends. I can share in a nonjudgmental environment my deepest sentiments, prayers, and aspirations. My close friends and I have laughed and cried together, and they have been strong supporters and challenge me in ways that stimulate growth. I hope that you also discover the joy in purposeful friendships and that the Lord would reveal to you those who will help you in this way.

Now let's talk about friendships with males (dun dun duuuun *sound effect*). You have probably heard the notion that great relationships start as friendships. While there may be some truth to that notion, I have found that it is wise to define friendships with males as soon as necessary. No, you don't have to lay out a list of ten commandments as soon as you meet a new male friend but don't be afraid to have a conversation to express your personal boundaries and intentions if the need arises. This mutual understanding helps to define the trajectory of the friendship and leaves no room for gray area or miscommunications.

If you two are just friends, then your conversations and interactions should not stray into deeply personal and emotional content. Even if you find yourself being attracted to a male who is only supposed to be a friend, be careful to not allow your emotions to drive the friendship into inappropriate territories or to initiate a pursuit.

I have also found it very important to be careful of how much information is shared with male friends. As emotional beings, women sometimes bare it all and wear their hearts on their sleeves too quickly. Deep details change the dynamics of a friendship. The oversharing of information too soon can turn into an attraction based on emotional vulnerability and not true love. Be wise about how soon and how much intimate information you share about yourself. Take the time to listen to the intentions and learn the character of a man before spilling your guts to him. Get to know who he is, what he values, and how he behaves in different situations without having deep emotional attachments that can cloud your judgement. That is what it means to build a friendship before venturing into a relationship.

Remember that friends are like elevators that either pull you up or push you down. The people that we have in our circles reflect our level of self-respect. Respect yourself enough to surround yourself with friends who portray good fruit and bring you closer to

God, not pull you away from Him. Grow deeper roots in those friendships and have conversations about the things that matter—about your deepest fears, about your ambitions, about your eternal security, about ways you both can pray for each other.

Use wisdom and discernment, in choosing your friends. Be sensitive to the season when friendships are no longer healthy and mutually beneficial and don't be afraid to let go of them. You don't have to wait until you are in a relationship to experience the joy of companionship. Friendships are a beautiful way to develop the qualities needed for a successful Godly marriage.

## Prayer

Father, thank you for giving me the discernment that I need to choose my friends wisely. Surround me with a supportive community who will encourage me in my faith and lift me up in prayer when I am weak. Please help me to show myself friendly so that I too can be the blessing of a Godly friend to someone else. Amen.

# CHAPTER FIVE

## *What Is Love?*

"Whoever does not love does not know God, because God is love." 1 John 4:8 (NIV)

What is love? Is it a feeling? A genre of movies and music? A genre of literature? So many of us grapple with such a simple yet profound question. But we cannot begin to explain love until the definition starts with *who* is love. The answer? God, of course! But how is love the very character and nature of God? Well, God expressed His love in the grandest way in the history of humankind. He gave His Only Son Jesus to die for our sins, our redemption, and our eternal security. We were once hopeless sinners, but Jesus died while we were still in our sin (Romans 5:8). There is absolutely nothing we can do to earn the gift of salvation that is available to us through Jesus. <u>It was love, not nails, that pinned Him to the cross.</u> Because of Him we are saved by grace through faith (Ephesians 2:8). There is no greater love than Jesus laying down His life for us, His friends (John 15:13).

## What Is Love?

Thus, we love Him because He first loved us (1 John 4:19). Once we come to understand and believe this, we are moved to love others because of God's love for us (1 John 4:11).

Love is more than just a mushy, fuzzy feeling that makes your stomach do somersaults or poetic rhymes that cause your heart to thud against the drum of your sternum. It is more than the cleverly crafted words of a song to make you feel like the only woman in the world. It is more than the butterflies you get when repeatedly reciting the name of your crush. It is more than gazing into the eyes of the man you are infatuated by and daydreaming about how many children you will have together.

Love is more of a choice than it is a feeling. Feelings are fickle but love does not change and has no end. Love is showing compassion, grace, and mercy to others even when you don't 'feel' like doing so. Love is treating people who dislike you with kindness. It is blessing people who curse you and praying for people who mistreat you. Love is giving of your time and resources to help someone in need, quickly forgiving when someone offends you and being patient with others. Love is sharing a kind word with a stranger, sharing your faith with an unbeliever, or giving your last dime to the person who came up short at the cash register. Love is caring enough to ask how someone is doing and intently listening to their response. It is esteeming another person as greater than yourself. Love is bearing one another's burdens, thinking about yourself less, and meeting the needs of others. Love is very practical and doesn't always feel warm and fuzzy. It is the choice to give, to care, to listen, or to pray even when you don't feel like it. First Corinthians 13:4–8 (NIV) tells us what love is.

> *Love is patient, love is kind. It does not envy, it does not boast, it is not proud. It does not dishonor others, it is not self-seeking, it is not easily angered, it keeps no record of wrongs. Love does not delight in evil but rejoices with the truth. It always protects, always trusts, always hopes, always perseveres. Love never fails.*

Learning to love others unconditionally as a single woman prepares you to also love sacrificially as a married woman. You can find practical ways to show your affection, appreciation, and care for your friends and family right now and I've got a few suggestions. Visit a neighbor when they are sick. Call a friend just to say that you are thinking about them. Cook a hot meal for your grandmother. Pay to fill your Dad's tank with gas. Spend time playing with your little brother. Have a heart-to-heart conversation with your sister. Celebrate the accomplishments of your best friend. Encourage your cousin to pursue his dreams. Give sound advice to a friend. These expressions of love teach you how to interact with others during both their high and low points of life. You learn to connect with those you love by doing the smallest things that make a big difference to them.

Find ways to love even the people who are "difficult" to love. The coworker who always complains, the mean supervisor, the pessimistic friend, and the uncle who doesn't share your beliefs all need love. Learn to treat these people with compassion and kindness. Pray for them so that the Lord can work in their hearts and their situations. Even when everyone else pushes them aside, be intentional about showing love to them. In the moment that you want to give up on them, remember that they need the same grace that God liberally and continuously extends to you.

Being able to love 'difficult' people through difficult situations is a test of unconditional love. It builds your patience and endurance to bear with others. Love is not always a good feeling. Just ask Jesus what it felt like to bear the sins of the world and be crucified. Sometimes sacrifices hurt. Sometimes selflessness is uncomfortable. But these experiences prepare you for unconditionally loving your future husband through every season of life—whether ill or healthy, rich or poor, for better or worse. That is what true, unconditional love is all about.

Loving others is just as important as loving yourself. In fact, the second greatest commandment, after loving God with our heart, soul, mind and strength, is to love our neighbors as we love ourselves (Mark 12:30-31). You cannot love anyone else if you do not love yourself. That means you must first take care of your spirit, mind and body. Listen to what your emotions are trying to communicate to you, be kind to yourself, and respect yourself. Love yourself enough to not allow others to mistreat you or force yourself to stay in unhealthy situations. Love yourself enough to let go of toxic people and not have your boundaries repeatedly violated. Love yourself enough to not ignore your needs while trying to keep others happy. It is only when you treat yourself with love that you will begin to treat your neighbors with love.

People often wonder about whether "love at first sight" is real; if it is possible to just know that one would spend the rest of their lives with a person after seeing them for the first time. While I do not dismiss the possibility of loving and marrying the person you were attracted to the first time you saw them, I hesitate to call it "love at first sight." To say that we are deeply and romantically in love with someone solely based on what we see is superficial because love is so much more than physical attraction. At first, second, or third sight, we are commanded to love our neighbors—anyone we come across—the way that we love ourselves. That is a brotherly type of love, but to be romantically in love at first sight is a little bit different.

The sight of a handsome man might make your heart skip a beat or take the breath out of your lungs, but does that mean you are in love with him? Perhaps a deep infatuation or a profound admiration. At first sight, you know nothing about the person besides the fact that they are physically appealing to you.

Love is a growing process, not something that you fall blindly into. It is cultivated by spending time with a person and being a learner of them. You may admire someone's eyes, intellect, sense of fashion, and humor at first sight. But the more you get to know about them and gradually connect spiritually, mentally, and emotionally, the deeper in love you *grow* with them.

Physical attraction may be enough to bring two persons together, exchange numbers, and perhaps even go out on a first date. But it is not enough to sustain a relationship because beauty is fading. Love is not contingent upon what a person looks like. Here's a test. If the person you are attracted to, even at first sight, were to get into a car accident and their face was mangled, would you still be able to love them in such a devastating condition?

People's faces will get wrinkles, their eyes will lose their sparkle, their hair will turn gray, their hairline will recede, and someday they will soak dentures in a cup. Can you still love them? Physical features are subject to change, and building a relationship solely based on appearance is dangerous. Anything can happen to our exterior, but love is sustained by what is on the inside. Even though society values a pearly white smile, flawless skin, and long straight hair, these things are bound to change. True love, however, will never grow old. It sees beyond the face and into the heart.

Besides the confusion of love with physical attraction, love has also been wrongfully associated with negative attention. Some women pass off disrespect and mistreatment as love because they genuinely do not know better. Maybe you have grown up without an example of true love. Maybe your parents abandoned you or you witnessed domestic violence as a child. Please understand that any form of disrespect, mistreatment, and abuse, are expressions of hatred that cannot coexist with love. No one who loves another person would intentionally inflict harm on them. A man who physically, sexually, mentally, emotionally, or verbally abuses or manipulates a woman is expressing his own insecurities in a weak effort to build himself up and prove his masculinity. (The same is true for women as well.) If you do not value yourself, then you will mistake mistreatment for true love. But true love should make you feel comfortable and secure. There should be no fear of abuse, manipulation, or exploitation because love is kind.

Now let's shift gears and talk about how the world views love. In a world where images of half-naked women sell cars and hamburgers, there is a common confusion between love and lust. We have grown to psychologically associate the value of a product with the sex appeal of the woman advertising it. The world is slowly growing desensitized to the prevalence of lust. Second Timothy 2:22 says we are to "flee from youthful lusts and pursue righteousness, faith, love and peace, with those who call on the Lord from a pure heart" (NASB). It is not a surprise that the Bible would tell us to flee from lust and pursue love. Love is pure. It is not tainted by ulterior motives and is not an untamed sexual passion. It does not objectify a woman or reduce her worth to her physical appearance.

Lust on the other hand usually starts as sexually inappropriate thoughts, and are manifested as untamed sexual desires. Lust leads us to sins like adultery, fornication, homosexuality and other sexual sins. Most times before things ever get physical, the sin has already occurred in our hearts. While it is not wrong to find someone physically attractive, disrobing and sleeping with them in your mind is the beginning of sexual immorality.

Lust must be addressed at the root of the heart because external sexual sin begins internally. "For it is from within, out of a person's heart, that evil thoughts come—sexual immorality..." Mark 7:21 (NIV). Living in a world that is excessively erotic, we should be certain to regularly perform a spiritual heart check up to discern the condition of our hearts. We should also rely on God to empower us to live the life He has called us to.

## What Is Love?

Our hypersexualized society has erroneously equated sex with love. But in the eyes of God, sex is merely an expression of love. It is not a boyfriend-benefit or a recreational activity. It was designed by God for us to enjoy according to His intentions, in the context of marriage. When we step out of bounds, we open ourselves to a world of unnecessary problems. Song of Solomon 2:7 charges us to "not to awaken love until the time is right" (NLT). But let's be real! Despite the potential consequences of unplanned pregnancies, sexually transmitted diseases (some of which are incurable), and soul ties associated with premarital sex, this is not an easy command to keep.

If you have already been sexually active, acknowledge that it was displeasing to God, ask for His forgiveness, and accept the grace that He lavishly extends. You are never too far gone to start doing things His way. It is never too late to start a journey of purity and celibacy. It will be one of the greatest gifts you can give your future husband to unwrap on your wedding night. Along that journey, you may meet men who try to push the envelope to see how far they can go until you finally break down or speak up. Do not be afraid to make your standards clear and stand unapologetically by them. Any man who challenges you on your standards of purity does not respect you and is most likely not your future husband. Your only recourse is to keep it moving!

Finally, true love is not for sale; it is not something you can walk into the store, pick up, and cash out. No one should be able to buy your heart through the purchasing of material things as genuine love gives without expecting anything in return. If a man tries to buy your body in exchange for handbags, some clothing, and jewelry, then those are gifts that you do not need. Elaborate gifts are major investments so be careful about accepting them. If he is expecting a sexual return on the investment before walking down the aisle, then the investment is being made in lust, not true love. Love will lead you to the altar first while lust will lead you to the bedroom first. Don't compromise your morals for money. Don't confuse love with luxuries. Don't give discounts on your dignity because your standards should never be negotiated.

I urge you to continue to live in the love of Christ as He pours out His love on you. Deepen your relationship with Him because to know God is to know true love. Until we know *who* love is, we will not fully understand what love is.

## **Prayer**

Jesus, thank you for being the perfect example of love when You died for me, even when my heart was far away from You. Please help me to find practical ways to love my neighbors the way that I love myself. I want to reflect You by the way that I serve others. Lord, during this season of my life, help me to draw closer to You because to know You is to know love. Amen.

# CHAPTER SIX

## *A Matter of Trust*

"Wait for the LORD; be strong and take heart and wait for the LORD." Psalm 27:14 (NIV)

"Trust in the LORD with all your heart and lean not on your own understanding: in all your ways submit to him, and He will make your paths straight." Proverbs 3:5–6 (NIV)

We live in a microwave era where we expect everything to happen instantaneously. Quick grits, instant noodles, five-minute oatmeal, frozen meals, online banking, on-demand television, hand dryers, weight loss pills and the list goes on and on. It is with that same surmise of immediacy that we pray for God to grant us the desires of our hearts. We want our prayers answered instantly without active preparation. Sometimes we pray prayers that are in alignment with our own desires instead of the will of God. We expect God to work on our timing and even become disappointed and disgruntled when the answer is "wait."

Waiting on God to answer your prayer for a husband can often be trying. It is easy to whine and complain when everyone else around you seem to get engaged and married before you. It is easy to stop praying and instead initiate your own pursuits. It is easy to give up on God when you think that He is not hearing your prayers, or to question whether He cares about your desires.

Waiting is not easy work! In fact, it becomes more difficult whenever you place your hope and your faith in anyone or anything else but God. It reminds us of how dependent we are on Him. When our hearts and desires are completely surrendered to the Lord, we have no other choice but to trust Him while expectantly yet patiently waiting.

Time is never wasted while waiting on God. He does His best work while we are waiting. The Lord doesn't just want to grant our desires but to also reveal His character as a good Father with perfect plans. He is more interested in using our waiting experiences to build our faith, increase our patience, remind us of our reliance on Him, and teach us to persevere in prayer. God doesn't cease to be good when He doesn't answer our prayers when we want Him to. His divine plans do not cease to be trustworthy.

The way that we respond to God's delay in granting our desires, is an indication of whether we believe or deny His goodness. In other words, our level of trust is revealed during our seasons of testing. Look at the story of Sarah and Abram. They waited for twenty-five years before God's promise for Abram to be the father of many nations was fulfilled. Ten years into the period of waiting, the elderly couple got impatient with God and concocted their own plan of conception. But Ishmael was not the promised child of God—Isaac was.

Now look at the Israelites who were led out of slavery in Egypt. It took them forty years of wandering in the wilderness before ever getting to the promised land—a journey that was only supposed to take a few weeks. During their period of testing, they grumbled and complained which led to a delay in their journey and some of them not even making it to the promised land.

In both examples, we see that waiting experiences are a testing period of faith and patience. Sometimes, like Sarah and Abram, we are tempted to devise our own plans to 'help' God. We begin to fret about how we will ever give birth to the promise or make it to our promised land. Our ungratefulness and impatience serve as hindrances because they shift our focus from the greatness of God to the bleakness of our situation.

When we begin to trust our own understanding, our faith and patience in God begin to diminish. But even when it seems like God hasn't heard our prayers, we must choose to patiently wait and prepare in expectation of Him moving on our behalf. This is the way that the glory of God is put on display—others will see us trusting in Him and they too will learn to put their trust in Him. Instead of complaining, give thanks. Encourage yourself with reminders of all the ways that God has answered your previous prayers. God has a track record of faithfulness and no matter how long He takes, He is always on time and delivers the superior gift.

The period of waiting is a time for God to prepare you for what you prayed for. There may be things that He needs to help you work through before revealing you to your husband. Maybe you still haven't gotten over an ex, or maybe you are holding on to issues of the past. Perhaps you still find it challenging to submit to God and obey His instructions. Maybe your priorities are misaligned and you spend your money, time, and resources carelessly. Perhaps you are too needy and expect a man to bring the wholeness and satisfaction that only God can bring. Maybe there is an underdeveloped area of your character that God is trying to perfect. Those are the issues that need to be surrendered to God. Wherever you are in this season, it is imperative that you activate your trust in Him and do not get weary in waiting.

As single women, we have to learn to not be envious of married women, but instead learn from them. Sit at their feet of wisdom and ask questions. Find out what it takes to have a successful marriage. Learn what it takes to resolve conflict, to raise children, and to balance the responsibilities of life. Gleaning from the wisdom and experiences of others is a pertinent part of actively waiting on the Lord. Allow the love stories of others to be an inspiration and a reminder that the same God who brought those couples together will someday unite you with your husband—and it will be worth the wait.

God doesn't only want you to trust Him with your love life. He requires total surrender in every area of your life. That includes your finances, job, academics, family, friendships, investments and everything else that is of concern to you. We sometimes tend to compartmentalize these areas in our hearts and only give Him partial access. But allow Him to have free reign in your life and you will see that the same God who pays your bills, writes your paychecks, and helps you to excel, is the same God who is faithful in preparing you to become a wife.

Your season of waiting and preparation all comes down to one question: "How much do you trust God?" Can you trust Him when He doesn't show you His plan, when you don't understand, when you feel weary, or want to give up? Whenever I start to feel impatient or anxious, I get in the presence of God and spend some time in worship. Those moments remind me of the faithful nature of God and how I need Him more than anyone or anything else. I am grateful that He not only wants to grant the desires of my heart but also wants to use my season of waiting for His glory.

Instead of sitting idly, I actively prepare for the things that I pray for. My attention is then shifted from my singleness to my service. I want God more than I want a husband. I am not only eager for God to do something *for* me but to do something great *through* me. When I personally arrive at this juncture I penned this prayer.

## Prayer

*Lord, I want to love You more than life itself. I want to need You more than I need my next breath. I want my desires to conform to Yours. I want to worship You like there is no tomorrow. I want to live my life poured out for Your glory. I want Your thoughts to permeate my mind and the thickness of Your presence to rest and abide with me. I want to experience You in a way that plunges me deeper into the truth of Your existence. With everything inside of me, I want to honor You. Hold my hand and whisper the assurance of Your unwavering love toward me. Teach me Your ways, order* *my steps. I want to be diminished along with the foolishness of my heart. I want You at the forefront of every facet of my life. I need You more than I need anyone or anything else. <u>I want to be so dependent on You that I am stagnant until I have Your stamp of approval.</u> I never want to become complacent where I am or be satisfied with a mediocre life. Keep pushing me, even if I get uncomfortable because that is when my faith in You grows the most. My life is not about me, but for the lives You will reach through me. Jesus, I just want to be emptied of myself so that each day I can take steps, no matter how small, toward You and the woman You have created me to be. I trust Your plans for every area of my life, and I surrender my will in exchange for Yours, knowing that Your timing is perfect. Amen.*

# CHAPTER SEVEN

## *Is It Well with Your Entire Well-Being?*

"So you also are complete through your union with Christ, who is the head over every ruler and authority." Colossians 2:10 (NLT)

The manufacturers of cars masterfully design them with features like tires, brakes, lights, mirrors, windshield wipers, and engines. These features work together to ensure the optimal functioning of the car. If you don't change a blown head light you will not be able to see at night. If you don't change your bald tires, there is an increased risk of losing control of the car and puncturing the tires. If you don't put oil in your engine, the friction from the rubbing parts will cause overheating. If any of the parts stop working the way they were designed to, the functional integrity of the entire car is compromised. In the same way, God has strategically created us as physical, mental, emotional, and spiritual beings all wrapped in one body. Each feature of our being serves a specific purpose and unless they are all functioning optimally, the quality of our lives and our well-being will be compromised. So, is it well with your entire well-being?

We all have the responsibility of taking care of ourselves—heart, mind, body and spirt. As wives in waiting, one of the greatest things we can do for ourselves is to become whole and to take care of every aspect of our selves. We often hear people say that to be healthy is to be wealthy. The reason that is true is because when you are healthy and whole, you are better able to help others become healthy and whole. You are better able to fulfill your purpose and make an impact on the lives of those around you. So, in what ways do you strive to be well?

Let's start with your physical well-being. Do you get enough exercise? How many glasses of water do you drink daily? Do you get enough sleep and manage your stress levels well? Are you attentive to the signs your body gives you when you get tired? I hope your answers to all the above questions were affirmative. If not, I hope that they have helped you to identify the ways that you can improve the self-care of your physical being.

Try doing something as simple as getting a manicure or a massage to help you to relax. Go to bed at a reasonable time. Make yourself a fruit smoothie. Take breaks throughout the day. Whatever you do, don't forget to be nice to yourself! No one can treat you better than you.

Let's talk about mental health—a topic that is oftentimes taboo. Challenges with mental health carry negative stigmas that need to be broken. Many women silently struggle with anxiety and depression whether diagnosed or undiagnosed. Our minds are constantly racing from the time we open our eyes in the morning to the time we rest our heads on a pillow at night. We think about the exhaustive list of things to do, errands we need to run, and deadlines that need to be met. Sometimes it can feel we are losing ourselves in the tasks instead of finding enjoyment in them. Maybe we start to get discouraged by the vicissitudes of life and find it difficult to make it through each day. My question to you is, how do you take care of your mental well-being? How do you unwind after a long day of work or school?

Do you journal, listen to music, or engage in your favorite hobby? Do you talk to others, read for leisure, or meditate? Are you in need of professional help to manage your mental health? Again, the objective is for you to think about the ways that you have been taking care of your mental well-being and to identify the ways in which you can improve. Be certain that you find healthy ways to release the thoughts on your mind. Learn to say "no" when you are not able to do something and don't make commitments that you cannot keep. Remember that you are not being selfish by taking care of yourself. It is a necessity.

As emotional beings, I don't think most women have an issue with staying in touch with their feelings. What we do with those emotions is what determines the state of our emotional well-being. Emotions are more than just our reactions to experiences in the world but are also indicators of the internal condition of the heart.

How do you express yourself when you feel angry, sad, happy, or afraid? Emotions are meant to be appropriately expressed—both the positive and negative ones. They help people to

*Wholeness in Singleness*

better relate to you and your experiences, and for you to also be able to communicate and connect with others.

Positive emotions deserve to be shared so that others can celebrate the goodness of God with us, as praise is rendered to His name. Likewise, our negative emotions also need to be expressed appropriately to avoid an implosion within ourselves or an explosion toward others. Since our emotions have an impact on ourselves and the people around us, we should practice appropriately expressing rather than suppressing them. We should invite others to share in both our joys and sorrows as we learn to give a voice to our feelings.

Finally, but most importantly is your spiritual well-being. If you are not spiritually well, nothing else in life will be well. Your spiritual well-being is like the fuel in your car. Even if all the other parts are functioning well, without fuel you still cannot go anywhere. Everything that you do is fueled by God. Your value, identity, and purpose all come from Him. All that you are and ever hope to be is because of Him. It is through Him that you live, move, and have your being (Acts 17:28). Nothing else in this world can satisfy you the way He can. You were created with a God-void—a hole that only He can fill.

Maybe you are at the point in your life where you have tried everything from sex to drugs to fill that void. Certainly, you would have found that those things have left you feeling more empty than before. Just like the temporal fixes that this world offers, relationships and marriage will never be able to fill the God-void inside of you. You are incomplete until you are made complete in

## Is It Well with Your Entire Well-Being?

Christ. Your spiritual well-being is pivotal to the health of your entire being.

By now you are probably asking "What does it mean to be whole through Christ?" The first step is to have a relationship with Him by receiving the gift of salvation. Upon salvation, we also receive the Holy Spirit who begins a new work on the inside of us. Our mind, will, thoughts, and emotions undergo a transformation as our lives begin to reflect Christ more and more. That transformation sets us on fire for the things of Christ as we seek to feed the spirit man and die to our flesh daily. The Lord then begins to reveal areas of our lives that He wants to work on, broken pieces He wants to mend, past baggage He wants to unpack, and poor habits He wants to break so that we can be more like Him. That is the process of becoming whole.

You can find wholeness in Christ no matter how broken and imperfect you are. Come to Jesus just as you are. Come with your tough life experiences and difficult background. Do not try to clean yourself up first because even your good works are as filthy rags before Him (Isaiah 64:6). God loves you so much and desires to be in an intimate relationship with you so that He can make you a new creature. If you are already in a relationship with Him, He wants to continue to fill every void in your life and mold you to bear His image.

I do not want you to think for a second that the journey to wholeness is going to be smooth sailing. An active relationship with Jesus is hard work! It is more than just saying a quick prayer in the morning and going about your day. Your relationship with Him is most fruitful when you are consistently seeking His face, reading and living His Word, and being obedient to the leading of the Holy Spirit. He shows you things about yourself and manifests Himself in the most amazing ways ever. The voice of God becomes consistent and clearer the longer you walk with Him. His joy and peace will fill your heart, and it is so comforting just to rest in His presence. But this takes time, sacrifice, and commitment.

The same way that you intentionally make lunch dates with friends and talk on the phone to catch up throughout the day, is the same way you can be connected with Jesus. Be intentional about being spiritually well and staying near to God. Build your life around Him. Surrender your mind, body, spirit, desires, emotions and will to Him so that you can be whole.

In my own journey to wholeness, I often cry out to God while taking showers, while driving alone, or while taking walks. Those are my quiet times to tell Him everything that is weighing on my heart and mind. I have found that no matter how physically tired, mentally exhausted, and emotionally drained I am, spending time in God's presence has a way of refueling my entire being. My anxieties are dismissed, my spirit is lifted, and I find rest in Him.

I want you to experience that same refueling through the building of an intimate relationship with God. When you become spiritually well, you will then have a solid foundation to ensure your entire well-being.

## **Prayer**

Lord, I realize that my wholeness in You is the foundation of my entire well-being. It is in You that I live, move, and have my being. I pray that You would help me to take care of every aspect of my being and that You would show me the areas that I have neglected. Help me to be self-aware so that I can conduct honest and complete self-care. Amen.

# CHAPTER EIGHT

## *The Purpose of Marriage*

"They are my people—I created each of them to bring honor to me." Isaiah 43:7 (CEV)

Here comes the bride, all dressed in white. With a bouquet of flowers in hand, you will someday walk down the aisle in the presence of God and witnesses to meet your future husband at the altar (if you have a church wedding). The second you utter the words "I do" your life will change forever. Those two small words will have such great meaning. You will give up the "me" in exchange for "we" as you become one flesh with your husband. You will agree that the only 'D word' that can separate you from him is death. Both of you will commit to staying with each other in the good and bad times. You will be there for each other whether healthy or ill, rich or poor. Those are some serious vows that come with hefty responsibilities and commitments that are not always glamorous.

## The Purpose of Marriage

The secondary benefits of marriage like companionship and procreation have been marketed by the media with little focus on its primary purpose. As single women, we are fixated on having a partner to help us make decisions, share financial obligations, and raise children. We long to have someone to come home to after a long day, to rub our feet and give us massages. We want to pour out our affections on our husbands, create lifetime memories with them, travel the world with them, and grow old with them. Those are all beautiful desires that are merely secondary benefits but not the primary purpose of marriage. God's design for marriage begins after the wedding, the white dress, flowers, and photos.

The primary purpose of the covenant of marriage is to model Jesus' relationship with His bride—the Church. He pursued, saved, sanctifies and eternally secured us. The way to model that type of love, commitment and sacrifice is for both husband and wife to continuously grow in their relationship with God and mature in Christ-like character. That character building process starts in the preparatory season of singleness. Without developing God's character, we cannot fulfill His purpose for marriage.

As we develop in character, marriage will serve as a mirror that constantly reflects our level of maturity in Christlikeness. We will be challenged daily as both husbands and wives are held accountable to each other. They are committed to love lavishly, to forgive frequently, to be patient persistently, to serve sacrificially, to help humbly, to resolve conflicts peaceably, to steward resources responsibly, and to submit respectfully.

Every day, your relationship with your future husband will require you to dig deeper into your relationship with God. Every day, you will have the responsibility of bringing to his attention his words and actions that are not Christ-like. Every day, you will be corrected in love as your future husband leads you to the things of Christ. Every single day, you will be challenged to bear the image of Christ for the primary purpose of God's glory.

That is the kind of love that cultivates a Christian home, which cultivates Christian communities and Christian nations. Eventually, the world can see the love of Christ being exhibited through the foundation of Godly marriages. This is a paramount purpose—the greater glorification of God through the unification of husband and wife.

Marriage is not a game. You cannot take a 'time out' or give up. You do not get a hall pass or a week off from marriage. It is a lifelong covenant that is too often trivialized. In today's world, we see the divorce rates skyrocketing as fifty percent of all marriages will be ended. What a saddening reality! For many of us, this reality is right at our front doors if not under our rooftops. Our close friends, parents, and family members may have gotten married and later divorced. There are several reasons that couples cite for divorce, but I can almost guarantee that those reasons are rooted in the misunderstanding of the purpose of marriage. Couples that do not have the right view of marriage will have the wrong pursuit of it.

Too many men and women buy into the benefits of marriage without understanding the biblical design of its functioning. Drawing reference to the car analogy once more, you may enjoy the benefits of the bluetooth radio and heated seats. However, if you don't know that its purpose of the car is to transport you from one location to another by starting the engine and driving it, then you would have invested thousands of dollars for a machine to sit in your driveway. Eventually, the features will get old and you may decide to *divorce* yourself from the car because you never understood how to optimize the purpose for which it was created. Overtime, the external beauty will no longer bring pleasure if the car cannot take you somewhere. In the same way, so many couples go from signing a marriage certificate to signing divorce papers.

We need to have the right view of marriage and realize that it was not designed to solve all our problems and fill all our voids. It is so much more than legal sex, creating cute babies and having a 'plus one' for black-tie events. Those secondary benefits get tired after a while. You will find yourself feeling broken, empty, and lonely even while lying in bed next to the husband you thought would fix and fulfill your life. But if you have the right view of the primary purpose of marriage, which is to mature in Christlikeness for the unified glory of God, then your marriage will never grow old. In fact, it will become more exciting as you are challenged to find new ways to serve, submit, build character, and be a helpmeet to your husband.

Now is the time to grow deeper in your relationship with Jesus and build the character that you need to have a successful marriage. Godly marriages have the potential to impact the world— a world that is straying away from His design and definition of marriage. You have the power to change the world just by saying "I do."

## **Prayer**

Lord, Your design for marriage is for the unified glorification of Yourself as we model Your loving relationship with the Church. Help me to pursue that primary purpose of marriage more than the secondary benefits. I want to follow Your design so that my marriage in the future can be a ministry that points others back to You. Amen.

# CHAPTER NINE

## *Grown Woman Dealing with Her Little Girl*

"But one thing I do: Forgetting what is behind and straining toward what is ahead, I press on toward the goal to win the prize for which God has called me heavenward in Christ Jesus." Philippians 3:13–14 (NIV)

There is a little girl inside of every woman, and it doesn't matter how old she gets, there are moments when memories of her come to mind. That little girl has had experiences that helped to shape the woman you are today. Maybe you have memories of her you wish you could hold on to forever and others you wish you could toss into the sea of forgetfulness. The latter are the memories which probably bear painful scars, still bring tears to your eyes, or has made your heart grow cold. Maybe you cry yourself to sleep some nights because no matter how hard you've tried, moving forward with baggage from the past seems impossible. Maybe it feels like trying to run through the airport with two huge suitcases and a backpack, to catch the final boarding call for your flight departing fifty gates away. The trot would

*Wholeness in Singleness*

be so much easier and faster if you did not have such a heavy load that slows you down.

If you can relate to those feelings, the unresolved issues of the little girl inside of you are like that luggage that stifle your growth, hinder you from maximizing your potential and impede the flourishing of your relationships. Ultimately, those same issues and baggage will be brought onboard the *flight* of your future marriage. If you do not take the time to unpack those issues, you are running the risk of crashing and burning because that load is simply too heavy to bear.

This is your captain speaking, "Come to me, all you who are weary and burdened, and I will give you rest. Take my yoke upon you and learn from me, for I am gentle and humble in heart, and you will find rest for your souls. For my yoke is easy and my burden is light" Matthew 11:28–30 (NIV). Jesus is inviting you to unload your baggage on Him in exchange for an easy yoke and a light burden. He is offering rest for your weary soul. He wants to unbox your burdens and rewrap you with liberty in Him. Singleness is not a season for dragging around past baggage and being consumed by the struggles of this life. It is time to check the load at the front desk as we unpack some of the real issues of the little girl on the inside.

## *Self-Image*

The objectifying women and the unrealistic standards of beauty have become so prevalent that it is very difficult for young girls not to question their self-image and worth. We have all done it—compared ourselves to a person on the magazine cover, tried a new diet to lose weight in ten days, or vigorously worked out every day for a week, then lost the motivation to continue. We have all compared ourselves to photoshopped images of airbrushed women. In our minds, we know that real women have beauty lines (stretch marks), wrinkles, dark spots, and maybe even a touch of acne. Yet still, we sometimes try to attain an unrealistic Barbie appearance that even supermodels and celebrities themselves spend thousands of dollars to achieve. Our society prizes women who are fair-skinned with long flowy hair, slender physique, curvy hips and plump lips as the standard of beauty. But the creative nature of God did not intend for us all to look that way. What about my natural hair sisters, those with a little more meat on their bones, and those of varying shades of gorgeous melanin? They are gorgeous too!

    Media has had a significant impact on the way we view ourselves. However, conforming to one ideal of beauty is an insult to the creativity of God when He uniquely made each of us in His image. It is time for us to embrace our true selves and be proud of the way that God has masterfully created us. While it is entirely acceptable to do things that enhance our beauty and boost our confidence, we've got to be certain that the motive for those efforts is to be happy and healthy, and not to conform to a beauty trend.

    The issue of internalized self-hatred is a very deep-seated one. We have been conditioned by the media and pop-culture to value some qualities and to put down others. Those who do not have the 'desirable' qualities often struggle with low self-esteem, eating disorders, and mental health issues because they don't 'meet the mark.' But we must remember that beauty comes in different colors, heights, shapes, sizes, and textures. Our standard of beauty should not be determined by societal norms.

Beauty is more than a social construct. It is an internal condition of the heart that is outwardly projected. It is more than just the numbers on your clothing tags or on a scale. Even more important than having a beautiful body is having a beautiful heart. It starts with your attitude, self-love, gentle spirit, wisdom, and character. Physical attractiveness is merely an additive to your inner beauty. With this understanding, our views of beauty and expressions of self then become an echo of what we believe about ourselves. Believe that you were created in the image and likeness of God—because you were! That is what makes you beautiful.

Love yourself and begin to see yourself the way that God sees you. Be happy and healthy. Be bold, be different. Be-YOU-to the full. Learn to love yourself first so that you don't have to depend on anyone else for validation and compliments just to boost your self-esteem. My sister, stop conforming to the image of others, and be who God has created you to be. I am certain that your future husband will love you just the way you are. You do not have to look like Beyoncé or the Kardashians to be beautiful.

If your childhood struggle with self-image has carried over into your womanhood, know that you are more than a number on a scale, a dress size, the length and texture of your hair, the height of your heels, and the makeup on your face. Beauty by God's standard says that you are wonderfully made from the inside out!

## *Passion*

What do Bill Gates, Oprah Winfrey, Steve Jobs, and Mark Zuckerberg all have in common? You may at once think that it is wealth and success. They have obtained the ownership of multiple businesses, private jets, mansions in various parts of the world, many cars, a computer software company, a television network, and a popular social media forum. These people we call celebrities and public figures have knowingly or unknowingly operated by the biblical principle of hard work to obtain such feats. The discovery of their passions has led them to great wealth and success. But as a believer, what is more important than achieving earthly success is using our passions to honor God.

Success is not measured by how many cars are in your driveway, how many degrees you've earned, the title plastered across your office door, having six-figure numbers in your bank accounts, or being world renowned for something. The true definition of success is how you use your influence, platform, expertise, opportunities, ideas, visions, education, gifts, and talents for a purpose greater than yourself.

As a child, you may have often been asked "What do you want to be when you grow up?" Your response may have ranged anywhere from a ballerina to a doctor. Maybe you have achieved that goal (which is amazing) or maybe you are still trying to figure it out. Now that you've grown up, there is an urgency to answer the question of "Why am I here?"

During this season of singleness, it is not only important to discover your purpose and passions, but also to further develop and operate in them. At the end of this life, you will give an account to God for the things that you did or failed to do (Romans 14:12). First Peter 4:10 says, "Each of you should use whatever gift you have received to serve others, as faithful stewards of God's grace in its various forms" (NIV). As a good steward of the passions and gifts that you possess, it is your responsibility to cultivate them in service to others for the glory of God. Someone is waiting for you to walk in your passion and purpose so that their life can be revolutionized.

I have heard stories of doctors and engineers who have spent thousands of dollars to be educated, only to realize that they are in a field that makes them unhappy. Some people end up in completely different fields like marketing, makeup artistry, or video blogging because that was where their passions were all along and the fields they were destined to be in. Don't try to live up to the expectations of others or push yourself into the careers that society has deemed prestigious. <u>Having the intellectual ability to do something does not mean that it is your purpose.</u> Everything you do should be in alignment with God's will for your life.

Find your path in life, and if it doesn't already exist, create it. "Seek his will in all you do, and he will show you which path to take" Proverbs 3:6 (NLT). Even more important than your profession is the discovery of your passion. Your profession should be rooted in your passion because your passion is rooted in your purpose.

Now is the best time to discover, cultivate, and operate in your passion and purpose. Let your future husband meet you pursuing God's purpose for your life. Please do not compare yourself to the feats of others and realize that there is more than one path to 'success.' Run your own race and whatever you wake up every morning to do, do it for the honor and glory of God. Do it not just for an income but to make an impact on the lives of others.

## *Rejection*

Has the little girl in you ever been rejected? Maybe she loved someone that did not love her back. Or maybe she is disappointed by people not being there when she needed them most. Maybe she grew up in foster care and struggles with the questions of "Am I loved?" or "Why didn't my parents want me?" Maybe she didn't get accepted on the soccer team or the dance squad. If you can relate, then you are probably carrying around very heavy baggage.

We were created with the need to be loved and we all want to feel appreciated—like we belong somewhere and to someone. Feeling rejected can often lead to one of two extremes—either complete isolation from others or unhealthy attachments to others. You may find yourself either closing your heart or overbearingly latching on to anyone who shows you love. Either you try to protect yourself from rejection by being very reserved, or you have an unrealistic expectation of perfection when you constantly attach yourself to someone or something. None of these circumstances are beneficial because it means that either you don't receive genuine love, or you idolize anyone or anything that gives love to you.

If you have a history of rejection, those are challenges that you need to face now. When you know who your acceptance comes from, you don't have to live with the fear of rejection. People may sometimes walk away from you but God has never walked out. Instead of rejecting you, He redeemed you. He thought you were worth pursuing with His love because you have such great value.

It is important to realize that when people leave you that they don't take your value with them. When you don't get the job that you want, it does not mean that you are not good enough. When you don't get accepted into the program you want to attend, it doesn't mean that you are any less qualified. It simply means that God has another plan that is better for your life so try to not take it personally.

Even though experiences of rejection hurt, you need to have faith that God's plan is better. Your rejection is God's protection from a toxic relationship, a mean boss, an unfair business deal, or a season that you have outgrown. Don't be afraid of rejection, rather see it as God's way of closing the doors that He doesn't want to be opened to you. When you begin to see rejection as a tool of protection, fear is removed. You will see that God is demonstrating His perfect love by the way He strategically orchestrates and allows things to happen in your life.

God wants to heal your heart from the scars of rejection with the consistency of His love and patience. He never leaves nor forsakes you even if your father and mother abandoned you (Psalm 27:10). Allow Him to swaddle you in His arms as you find love, value, and acceptance in Him. Whenever you begin to feel rejection, remind yourself of the scripture in 1 John 3:1 that says "See what great love the Father has lavished on us, that we should be called children of God" (NIV). God loves you so much that He considers you His daughter. He has already wrapped His arms around you and claimed you as His own. God never has and never will leave you!

## *Depression*

Depression is one of the heaviest forms of baggage that a person can carry. It feels like you are drowning in an ocean of hopelessness without the ability to swim to the shore of a bright future. It feels like you are being consumed by darkness and being sapped of all your energy to fight. Smiles are facades to hide the pain, and rolling out of bed in the morning is the most difficult part of the day. Depression is a mental paralysis, physical numbness, and an emotional hurricane. She who feels it knows it, and I too have felt it. Here is a journal entry from 2010 at a point in my life when I was feeling depressed and having one of "those days."

> *Those days when you feel so out of it and empty you want to cry but do not have the tears. When you want to be close to someone yet simultaneously want to be left alone. Those days when you feel emotions that you cannot put into words, yet you cannot deny their existence. Those days when you long for relief but cannot see the light at the end of the tunnel. Those days when you want to lay in bed and stare at the ceiling, because you don't have the motivation to do anything else. Those days when you compare yourself to others and wonder where you went wrong. Those days*

*when you so deeply desire to have genuine happiness but don't know where to turn. Those days when you stop pretending to have it all together because on the inside you are falling apart. Those days when even the simplest things irritate you because you are miserable and moody. Those days you want to wallow and allow the pen to bleed out the troubles of your heart. Those days when you don't know how to pray or don't have the fortitude to read the Bible but you know how much you need God. Those days when you feel like you did your best and gave your all but it still wasn't good enough. Those days when you wonder what more you could have done even after feeling like you've done all that you can. Those days you worry about your future and how you can possibly make it out successfully from your current situation. Those days when you are in a desperate search for God but He seems to be far away. Those days when you encourage others but you are crying out for encouragement, for motivation, for a reason to keep pushing. Those days when you try to cling to the last bit of hope left within you. Those days when you feel there is no one who truly understands you and it is simply too much of a hassle to even begin to explain the emotions you feel. Those days when you are strong for others, but you need someone to be strong for you.*

*Yes, I'm having one of "those days." But amid it all, it is on these days that God keeps me and I hold on to His promise to never leave nor forsake me. I know that God understands my groans of a prayer. I put my hope in Him because He is the only one who can uplift me. These are the days when everything within me yearns to draw close to Him so that*

*He can be the glory and lifter of my head. These are the days when His strength is made perfect in my weakness.*

Depression is a mental battle and you've got to have the right weapons to fight it. At those low points of your life, you may barely have the words to pray or the strength to read your Bible. With all that is within you, you've got to hold on to hope and faith and keep fighting. I was only able to cling to hope and faith because the Word of God was already hidden in my heart and I had something to draw on. In those low times, I reminded myself of scriptures about God's promises to never leave me and to be my joy. When the Enemy attacks us with Depression, he is trying to deceive us into believing that we are alone and hopeless. But the best weapon that we have to combat depression with is the Word of God.

The most detrimental outcome of depression is suicide and that is exactly what Satan would want. John 10:10 says, "The thief comes only to steal and kill and destroy; I have come that they may have life, and have it to the full" (NIV). The Enemy wants to steal your joy, destroy your mind, and literally take your life. He wants to see you mentally deteriorate to a state of hopelessness and worthlessness; to the point where you take your eyes off God and zoom in on your problems.

If the Enemy can control your mind, he can control your life. Your mind is a battlefield, and every morning you must wake up determined to fight. But you cannot fight alone and in your own strength. The same power that raised Jesus from the dead, lives within you. You have power over the Enemy! You have power over depression. Speak life over situations that seem hopeless and dead. Rebuke the schemes and plans of the Enemy. Go into warfare. Worship your way through. Whatever you do, DON'T GIVE UP!

With God on your side, you never have to shoulder burdens on your own. Tell someone you trust; there is someone willing to listen, who cares, who understands, who will believe you, who will pray for you, who will walk with you. Combat the lies of the Enemy with the promises in the Word of God. Here are a few: Romans 8:37–39, Philippians 4:19, Isaiah 40:29–31, and Jeremiah 29:11. Continue to feed your spirit so that you have the power to overcome depression.

Whether your depression stems from learning of an illness, the loss of a job, stress from school or work, a disappointment, personal failure, family issue, new stage in life, or a death, remember that there is light at the end of the tunnel! Life is a combination of peaks and vallies that all miraculously and strategically work together for our good and God's glory. It takes serious faith to believe that!

I understand that depression can be a clinical diagnosis, and there is nothing wrong with seeking professional help from a Psychologist or Psychiatrists or talking with someone you trust. God has given those people the wisdom and knowledge to help bring your suppressed issues to the surface so that you can confront them. You may have been depressed all your life, but today can be the beginning of a new life filled with joy in Christ.

These areas are strongholds that may have been in your life since you were a little girl. There may even be others that I failed to mention. It is time for you to check all the baggage you have been carrying around at the front desk and leave them there. A huge part of the journey to wholeness is your ability to let go of your past, or any situation that is stunting your growth.

Many of us continue to blame our current state of brokenness on the incidents and experiences of our past. We continue to hold on to those incidences as crutches and excuses for not being well. It is natural to feel hurt, angry, frustrated, or disappointed about the misfortunes in life. But at some point, the conscious decision must be made to pick up the pieces with the help of God and move toward wholeness.

Too many of us use our pain to justify our sin or justify character flaws by saying "that's just the way I am." But you don't have to be bitter, angry, Depressed, moody, or defeated. Change is difficult but necessary. The challenging circumstances of life are not good excuses to avoid undergoing the healing process. So many of us have gotten familiar with pain and allowed those difficulties to define us. But let me tell you that you may not have control over the past, but with the help of God, you can create a new path into the future.

It is time to stop making excuses. Stop living a defeated, broken, and unhealthy life and come find joy and wholeness in Christ. He is the only One who can fill those empty spaces and mend those broken places. He is the only one who can help a grown woman deal with her little girl.

The prayer for this chapter is an open letter that I wrote to my past. I was struggling with acceptance, pride, unforgiveness, and depression. The letter starts with brokenness but ends in beauty. I want to use the state of brokenness that I was once in, to inspire you to bring your burdens to the Lord and find wholeness in Him.

## Prayer

*Dear Past,*

*That is exactly what you are! Distant memories flash ever before me on the monitor of my mind. When I look back at you I can recall how broken and empty I used to be—looking to the things and people of this world to complete me. Your soundtrack of sadness used to serenade my heart. You are as convoluted as a treble clef that preceded melodies of negative emotions. I hated the way you robbed me of my confidence and the way my mind became a receptacle for your haunting recollections. My mind became a battlefield as I fought internally to find peace, wholeness, and happiness. Every day I chose not to let you go, frustration built up on the inside. I got tired of carrying the weight of the ball and chain of misery you left around my heart. Emptiness never felt so heavy, and bitterness never tasted so poisonous. I once lived behind self-constructed walls of fabricated perfection and a façade of "togetherness" when I was just one shake away from complete brokenness. I became accustomed to living with pain that served as a constant reminder that I needed help! I was broken and I knew that only Jesus could fix me.*

*Today you have been served a letter of eviction from your habitation in my mind. All the guilt, anger, frustration, bitterness, depression and defeat—I now choose to release them. Effective immediately, you will no longer have control over my life, my mind, my heart or my emotions. You do not dictate the trajectory of my life because I choose to charter a course of joy, courage, forgiveness, hope, and wholeness. Thank you for the wisdom and strength you have given me and the countless life lessons you have taught me. Now I embark upon a promising future in Christ Jesus, as I seek to become whole in Him. To you, the past, I say "good riddance!"*

*Sincerely,*

*No Longer Yours Truly*

# CHAPTER TEN

## *Daddy Issues*

"See what great love the Father has lavished on us, that we should be called children of God!" 1 John 3:1 (NIV)

I have been blessed to have a father who plays an active and integral role in my life. The love I have for him is so profound and I wish every woman could experience that kind of relationship. The type of bond that a little girl has with her father has a significant impact on her view of self, her relationships with others, and her expectations of other men. Every little girl needs her father to reaffirm her value, and to remind her of her inner and outer beauty. She needs her dad to show her what it means to be treated respectfully by other men. She needs him to be a support system, to correct lovingly, and to guide gracefully. She needs his provision, protection, love, and affection. We need our daddies to tell us to dream big, to be our figures of authority, to teach us to be disciplined and obedient. We need them to be the priest of our homes, and to remind us that our worth comes from God and not our bodies or our boyfriends. Every little girl deserves to spend quality time and play time with her father. And even when he humanly falls short, she needs him to acknowledge his shortcomings and to keep striving.

  Daddy issues are becoming too common today as more and more homes are devoid of fathers. The reasons why fathers are absent from the home range from custody battles, to incarceration, and alternative lifestyles. Some fathers are physically present yet emotionally unavailable, and others have multiple households to support.

  For whatever reason your father was absent, please know that it was not your fault. Allow me to show you something from a different perspective. I do not know the circumstances that your dad was in, but have you considered that he may not have known how to be a father to you? Have you considered that his dad may have also walked out on him, or that no one ever taught him the responsibilities of fatherhood? Maybe your dad was not in the best condition to parent you because of an addiction. Maybe he felt inadequate to fulfill his role as a father. Maybe you both were separated by unfortunate situations or physical distance.

  Whatever the reason for his absence, it would have been extremely difficult for him to emulate what he has never seen, or to do what he was never taught. If he was not his best self, then he may not have been the best father that you needed. He could not have given you what he did not have, and it takes a lot of maturity on your part to even begin to consider his perspective.

Maybe your dad was present but never told you how much he loves you, or maybe he left you sitting on the front porch for days at a time before you saw him again. Maybe he only sent a check in the mail, while you were longing for his time and presence in your life. But none of this changes the fact that your heavenly Father was there all along.

He knows how much you are hurting as an adult and how much you long for the answers to so many questions. He knows that your heart was broken when you watched your mother struggle to keep food on the table and clothing on your back. But you know what? God made a way. He brought you this far, not to leave you, but to continue to take care of you in ways your father was not able to. Allow Him to fill the void for your earthly father with His consistent love and faithfulness.

Many of the insecurities that single young women struggle with are rooted in daddy issues. The search for a father in boyfriends, the clingy and codependent nature of relationships, trust issues, the fear of being alone, the attachment of self-worth to relationships, feeling unlovable, anti-social behavior, and having a need to be constantly reassured of other people's love can all be connected to daddy issues. These insecurities will oftentimes spill over into every area of our lives if we do not deal with them directly. What better time to address them than now? You deserve to have resolutions and closure to the pain of your past.

The first thing that you should do is acknowledge the ways your father's absence has affected the things that you have come to believe about yourself and your relationships with others. Maybe you tend to be possessive, have difficulty making and keeping friends, have dated emotionally-absent men, or have difficulty trusting people. Whatever your symptoms, write them down along with the narratives that you tell yourself.

Combat those negative beliefs about you being unlovable, or about not being worthy of companionship with positive affirmations and truths found in the Word of God. Continuously remind yourself that God never left you, that your value is found in Him, and you are special to Him. Only He knows why the situation with your father played out the way that it did. Perhaps your father's presence would have been even more painful than his absence. Trust that the Lord has a strategic plan for even the painful parts of your life and that it is for your good. Push out the negative thoughts and replace them with the truth.

The second thing that you should do is forgive your father for the deep-seated pain that he caused you. I know, I know! Forgiveness is not easy, but it is an absolute necessity for your own freedom. It is the conscious decision to let go of his offenses against you, to not hold a grudge, and to move forward.

This forgiveness may move you to reconnect with your dad and pursue an adult relationship based on mutual respect. He may have missed a lot of your childhood milestones and accomplishments. You may not need him to pay your tuition or cook you breakfast anymore, but he may be able to offer moral support or give you a word of wisdom based on the experiences he has had. Embrace the possibility of a mature relationship with your father if he is willing, if it is healthy, and if it is the Lord's will. Such a reconnection can help you to understand yourself and become the best version of yourself.

If you do not know who your father is and would like to have a relationship with him, I encourage you to reach out to a professional, your mom, extended family members, or family friends who may have an idea of where he can be found. The process is tedious but can very well be rewarding. Keep in mind that you may not get all the answers you want, but at least you will have the satisfaction of trying. Should you and your father reunite in a healthy relationship, it would be a beautiful display of God's healing power and a testimony of how He can mend broken situations.

If for some reason, it is not at all possible or healthy to be reconnected with your dad, pray for the Lord to show you a man who can be a father-figure in your life. It may be an uncle, pastor, or an older relative that you trust to give Godly counsel. He should have an upstanding character, be a man of integrity, and a role model of what it means to be a leader, nurturer, provider and protector.

You should also pray for your father—for his salvation and relationship with Jesus. Pray that the Lord would fill his voids and help him to fulfill the purpose for which he was created. Most of all, know that God is the greatest Father that you can ever ask for and He will always be at your side. He created you and loves you as His daughter. Allow Him to heal your broken heart and free you from every negative emotion.

When I realized the burden of the absenteeism of fathers on our society, I was stirred to write a poem. Here are the last few stanzas of that piece and I hope it encourages you.

*To the daughter whose earthly father is absent, you deserve better*
*Allow me to introduce you to a Dad who promises to leave you NEVER*
*You are not fatherless; in fact, you have the best Father in the world*
*No matter how young or old you are, He's proud to call you His girl*

*For every female who is growing up or grew up without her dad,*
*For every tear you've shed and day you've dread because you were sad,*
*For every insecurity and fear that someone else in your life would leave,*
*For every hardship you've courageously endured and secretly grieved*
*I have just a few words of wisdom and encouragement for you*
*You are loved, you are peculiar, you are valuable, and precious too*
*Only one person can heal your heart, so make Him the center of your world*
*He has never left because you are and will always be God's (Daddy's) girl*

## Prayer

Lord, my heart is broken because of the absence of my father as a child. It feels like I have been deprived of something I deserved. Please reassure me of Your constant love and fill that void. I pray that if my father doesn't know You, he would he would come to accept You and experience Your love and grace. Lord, if it is Your will that we should be reunited, I pray that You will open the door to a healthy and fruitful relationship. I ask that You please give me the strength to not only forgive my father but to also walk in love and forgiveness. I surrender my insecurities to You now and exchange them for the fullness of Your joy and peace. Amen.

# CHAPTER ELEVEN

## *Soul Ties*

"'And the two will become one flesh.' So they are no longer two, but one flesh." Mark 10:8 (NIV)

Have you ever seen the potato chip commercial that tells you it is impossible to eat just one and be done? Maybe you have even tried them. As soon as the potato chip lands on your tongue your taste buds explode and you immediately have a craving to eat another. Soon you pop one potato chip after another until the entire bag is empty, yet you wish there were just one more left. Maybe you think about opening another bag because they were just that delicious. Well, what if I told you that soul ties work the same way? Once you've had a taste of intimacy with a person whether sexual or non-sexual, you begin to crave for more and more of them. Maybe they begin to consume your thoughts and emotions as you develop a deep desire to be with them. These ties can be formed with a significant other, a parent, a best friend, a co-worker, an authoritative figure, or anything or anyone with whom you share a personal connection. Some of them are healthy and others can be unwholesome, and it is very important to know the difference. Soul ties can either make you or break you because relationships have a significant impact on your thoughts, feelings, and desires.

The soul consists of the mind, will, emotions, and desires of a person, and a soul tie can connect you to another person through these same avenues. They are created in the spiritual realm long before they ever become sexual, emotional or verbal. To avoid creating unnecessary soul ties, all of our interactions should be spiritually discerned because the Enemy duplicitously tries to derail us from our destiny by using the people closest to us to form ungodly soul ties. For those of us who have accepted Jesus as Savior, the Holy Spirit dwells on the inside of us. When our minds, wills, emotions and desires are connected to the Spirit of God, we can then discern which connections are wholesome and which are unhealthy.

Soul ties in marriage are healthy because they keep the husband and wife together as one—wanting each other's 'potato chips.' That tie is initiated when the married couple consummates through sexual intercourse and become one flesh spiritually. That is why soul ties outside of this intended context bring about unhealthy connections to other people. That is why one night stands, *stand* longer than a night. That is one of the reasons why the Bible commands us to abstain from premarital sex. It is more than just sex with a body, but the intertwining of souls. Multiple soul ties make for a fragmented soul because they are easy to make but difficult to break. You will never realize how attached you are to another person until trying to sever ties with them.

Besides fornication, sexual soul ties can also be formed through adultery, homosexual activity, any form of sexual assault, or pornography. These activities can illegitimately and immorally tie you with the soul of another person, whether willingly or forcefully, and create access to all the curses in their bloodline. These ungodly ties can become avenues that the Enemy uses to try to destroy your life and keep you bound by lustful appetites, perverted desires, and addictions that can never be fully satisfied. But thanks be to God who has the power to set us free. Jesus has the power to break chains and ungodly soul ties.

Some years ago, I had an unhealthy soul tie to a friend who I knew was draining me emotionally, mentally, and spiritually. Although there were some good times, we had a lot of intense disagreements, and constantly walked on 'pins and needles' to avoid the next passive-aggressive remark. I felt unsupported in my endeavors, emotionally manipulated, and I was constantly working to 'fix' things even when I knew I was supposed to be letting go of the friendship.

It took me about two years to completely sever all ties with that friend and I cannot say I was eager to do so. Deep inside, God had been dealing with me on the situation. For a very long time, I was disobedient to His voice. I thought someday it would all get better and we would have grown out of that 'phase.' But now I realize that the friend was only in my life for a season and the longer I held on to that friendship after the season had expired, the more toxic it became. We grew further apart and my disobedience drew me further away from God. I have since proven the adage to be true that obedience is better than sacrifice. I could have saved myself a lot of stress and heartache had I just obeyed the Lord when He spoke the first time.

Another type of soul tie that single women often make is an emotional soul tie, particularly with male friends. These soul ties are not sexual in nature but can still be unhealthy if they are spiritually unguided. Every time we open ourselves and become vulnerable about our inner thoughts, personal struggles, intentions, and deep desires, a connection can be made. While transparency is essential for building community, accountability, and support, being vulnerable with someone who should not have deep access to the heart can be dangerous. While it is not wrong to be honest about your feelings or struggles, be wise about how much information you share and with whom you share it. Everyone does not deserve access to the depths of your heart so be prudent.

One type of soul tie that we don't often talk about is the one formed by words. If you've ever heard the saying "My word is my bond" then you will understand that words tie us to other people. When you say things like "I will never leave you," or "You will always be the one for me," you tie yourself to another person. Again, this may or may not be a healthy bond. In the case of wedding vows, words tie us in Godly covenants. But in the instances of broken friendships or relationships, any ungodly oath or promise bind you to the other person. These ungodly ties make it difficult for you to let go of the person if things turn toxic. The essential point is that there is truly power in your tongue so let your words be spiritually discerned.

If you are still uncertain whether you have an unhealthy soul tie, let me give you some vital red flags. Manipulation, possessiveness, obsession, jealousy, over-dependency, abuse, confusion, and adoption of the person's negative traits are all indicators of an ungodly soul tie. You may also experience drastic mood changes based on whether the person is around you. Perhaps, you may require their approval of everything you do. You may have a deep yearning for sexual activity with them. Or you may be willing to hold on to them at all cost despite the toxicity of the relationship.

Most times you will get an uneasy feeling about the relationship but maybe you have been ignoring the leading of the Holy Spirit because your desires do not align with His will. Don't try to manipulate the situation to appease your flesh and its desires. Don't deceive yourself into thinking that you can force the other person to change. The fear of the pain associated with letting go can leave you going through cycles of ungodly soul ties. But consider the greater cost of disobedience. Your failure to let go of an ungodly soul tie can cause you to miss your soul mate.

If you have ungodly soul ties in your life, I challenge you to trust the voice of God and let them go. Maybe you have tried on your own to be separated from the person (or thing). Perhaps you have only been able to separate from them for about a week or two before running back to them. Maybe you feel like you cannot go through life without them. Newsflash: Yes, you can!

It does not matter how many sexual partners you have had or how long you have been in a relationship or friendship. Those unhealthy ties can be broken. You need God's strength to make a conscious and consistent decision to break all contact with a person and to say "no" every time an opportunity presents itself to reconnect the two of you illegitimately.

Renounce that relationship and break any agreements you made with the person. Get desperate and do whatever it takes! Return the material things that trigger thoughts of your experiences with the person. Discard photos and cards that remind you of them. Remove them from your contact list and social media forums. It takes you continuously starving your flesh and being intentional about purging your soul by renewing your mind in the Word of God. Spend time in the presence of God and allow Him to fill that empty space and make you whole again. Pray for deliverance from any ungodly spirits and curses that were made accessible to you through ties with that person. Ask someone you trust to hold you accountable during your process of detox.

Once the tie has been broken, you do not need to keep checking the person's social media pages to see how things are going in their life. You do not need to keep rereading old text messages, replaying old voice notes, and crying yourself to sleep over what once was, because that person is not a part of your destiny. Sometimes seeing the photos and hearing their voices can be enough to take you back to the very situation you are trying to detox from. Be proactive, and do not give the Devil an opportunity to resuscitate a connection that needs to remain dead.

The most important precaution that you can take is to avoid making unhealthy soul ties instead of later having to break them. That requires you to be spiritually discerning of anyone who comes into your life. The Enemy will try to find ways to reconnect you in unhealthy soul ties, even if it is with someone new. Keep your eyes and ears open to the spoken and unspoken red flags associated with other people. Sharpen your ability to determine right from wrong based on your previous experiences, the Word of God, and the Holy Spirit dwelling within you.

As you take practical steps to move forward, be intentional about replacing the void of a lost friendship or relationship with something constructive. Maybe the soul tie drew you away from Bible study or the church. Reconnect yourself with the things of God and the things you enjoy doing. Rediscover a hobby or start a new one. Ultimately, you must choose to believe that God's will is better than your own, and then be obedient to the leading of His Spirit. Focus your attention less on what you will give up and more on what you will gain through your obedience. Change can sometimes be uncomfortable but growth can never happen in comfort zones.

## Prayer

Father, I pray that You would forgive me for consciously engaging in any ungodly soul tie and forgive the person who forcefully created a soul tie with me through any form of abuse. In the name of Jesus, I renounce and cancel every unhealthy connection and demonic plan. I declare that my soul is free from the soul of (__insert name__) and any ungodly spirits, strongholds, curses, and agreements that illegitimately entered my life through this connection. I pray for the person(s) that I am breaking free from and that You would also destroy any satanic plans in their life. Please give me courage as I am obedient in taking practical steps in walking away from this relationship/friendship. I pray for the spiritual discernment to only make connections with people who will be a positive influence in my life. Thank you for freeing me. Amen.

# CHAPTER TWELVE

## *Lonely but Not Alone*

"Be strong and courageous. Do not be afraid or terrified because of them, for the LORD your God goes with you; He will never leave you nor forsake you." Deuteronomy 31:6 (NIV)

So, Valentine's Day rolls around and you've got the Sulkers Starter Kit ready, complete with a pint of ice cream, sad chick flick movies, sappy love music, a box of Kleenex, and a blanket. You sit in your bedroom all day crying about the fact that you do not have a boyfriend, no one will take you out to dinner, buy you chocolates and flowers, or write you a sweet card. You feel like a complete loner, unloved, and not special. After all, what woman would not want to be cuffed on Valentine's Day, right? Everything begins to irritate you, from the colors red and pink, to the overheard conversations about date plans, to the soppy commercials on television. You are tempted to take one of the guys out of the friend zone for a week or two, just so you can join in the festivities and not be tthat' girl. I've been there before, and I remember those feelings all too well. (Now I can laugh at myself). Scrolling down my timeline would have been enough to get me *in my feelings*. But I have since learned to be in my faith and trust the Lord to honor my desires and write my love story.

It is natural to want to be loved and feel appreciated by a significant other. But it is also important to remember that everything is beautiful in its time. The season you are in right now is beautiful and it is up to you to find happiness while single. Don't allow yourself to mope around the house and complain about not having a date. Be your own date! Set a candlelight dinner and cook for yourself. Buy your own flowers, and go get your nails and hair done. Buy your own chocolates, and take a trip to the spa. Go travel the country with your single friends and relatives, and try a new food or activity.

Live life to the fullest and love yourself! Get together with other single women and share a day of love and laughter. Host a movie night with pillow talk and popcorn. Your life doesn't have to be boring. Find the beauty in singleness and celebrate this time. You have the freedom to travel, to make impromptu plans, and to try new adventurous activities. Maximize those freedoms!

As you find ways to add color to your single life, I do not want you to run off with the idea that hobbies can make you whole and recreation can make you complete. Those are merely activities that help you to maximize your time. Of course, there will inevitably be moments when you humanly feel lonely and desire to be married. It's okay to feel that way from time to time, but how you handle those feelings are paramount.

Many of us spend our entire single (and married) lives running away from the feeling of loneliness by filling it with entertainment, social media, and other activities. While being occupied and having fun is healthy, we must also learn to be okay with being by ourselves from time to time. The external activities that we use as coping mechanisms may bring temporal joy to our hearts but can never permanently satisfy us. That is because we were created with a God-void.

No relationship, party, movie, sport, or hobby will ever be able to take the place of God in our lives. If we don't run to Him to fill us up, we will realize that our activities become mere distractions from the fact that we were created with the desire for someone greater than ourselves. That is why loneliness is not altogether a terrible thing. It is God's way of beckoning us to come find wholeness in Him and spend time with Him. So how do you handle that feeling? Do you run to God or away from Him?

Whenever I feel lonely, I spend time writing poetry, journaling, and writing letters to my future husband. I allow the words of my pen to become prayers to God. I ask Him to help me find contentment in His presence and to satisfy my soul. That doesn't mean that my desire to be married is disregarded, it is surrendered. I have come to realize that absolutely no person or activity can satisfy me the way that God can.

In your moments of loneliness, remember the words of Jesus, who said in Matthew 28:20 who said "I am with you always, even to the end of the world" (AKJV). Even though we may feel lonely, we are never alone. Instead of sitting around and crying let's be productive for the kingdom. There are so many ways that we can serve as single women. Find something that interests you whether working in a soup kitchen, mentoring a young girl, volunteering at an animal shelter or joining a ministry at your church.

Whenever you start to feel lonely, remember that loneliness is God's way of getting your attention to spend time with Him. Without the distractions of television, friends, social media, and cellphones, quiet yourself before Him, spend time in His Word, and hear what He has to say. Know that it does not matter how long it takes for your future husband to come along; he will, and it will be beautiful in its time.

We need God more than we need anyone or anything else. He is the only one that can satisfy our voids and can grant us the desires of our hearts. Let's allow Him to fill us up as we find contentment in Him. He will exchange our loneliness for complete wholeness.

## Prayer

Jesus, nothing in this world can ever satisfy me the way the You can. Help me to not use activities of recreation and entertainment as distractions from my need to spend time with You. Help me to embrace loneliness as the tool that You use to draw me closer to You. I want to maximize this season to find contentment in You and to be productive for Your kingdom. Amen.

# CHAPTER THIRTEEN

## *The Anguish of Anger*

"Better to live in a desert than with a quarrelsome and nagging wife." Proverbs 21:19 (NIV)

As human beings, we all get upset from time to time and feel the need to voice our concerns. Anger is a normal human emotion that often communicates to others that we are displeased or may even cause us to spring into action during the proper context. However, feeling angry from time to time is different from being an angry person. Anger that is uncontrolled and excessive can become destructive in every area of your life. It may negatively impact your performance at work, relationships with co-workers, family, and friends, your well-being, or the quality of your life. If you find yourself intensely angry, for long periods of time, frequently, and for inappropriate situations then you may have issues managing your anger. This is not a clinical diagnosis but an effort to show you how destructive extreme and uncontrolled anger can be.

*Wholeness in Singleness*

Anger in and of itself is not a sin. But when we allow it to cause us to respond inappropriately to a situation, it becomes a sin. Sinful anger comes about when we say things with the intent to hurt another or commit actions with the intent of destruction or revenge. Ephesians 4:26-27 says, "Be angry, and yet do not sin; do not let the sun go down on your anger, and do not give the devil an opportunity" (NASB). Sinful anger is driven by hatred and causes us to behave senselessly with the goal of getting back at the offender. It will send you to bed weighed down, only to wake up even more upset, plotting your execution of revenge. But God says in Romans 12:19 "I will take revenge; I will pay them back" (NLT)

Godly anger, on the other hand, is driven by love. I know it seems paradoxical for anger and love to be used in the same sentence. But the intent of Godly anger is not to take revenge but to correct, to redirect, to stand up for what is right while allowing God to rain on both the just and the unjust (Matthew 5:45). He doesn't need your help in executing justice no matter how upset you may be. Our definition of justice may look very different from God's definition. Sometimes we want people to hurt as much as we do but that kind of anger is more destructive to us than it is to the offender.

If you have sinful anger in your heart, ask yourself what is the root of that anger. From that angry root, you may have noticed the fruits of unforgiveness, grudges, malice, and resentment. Maybe you are still bitter with your dad for not being in your life. Maybe you are still hurt about your rights being violated. Maybe you are still upset at the rude comment someone made. Whatever the source of your

## The Anguish of Anger

anger, your joy, peace of mind and well-being depends on your forgiveness.

Forgive the person that hurt, betrayed, misled, neglected, or cheated on you. Forgive the person who insulted you, spoke down to you, or gave up on you. Forgiveness is for you—for your sanity, freedom, and healing. It is for you to be able to sleep at night. Matthew 6:15 "But if you do not forgive others their sins, your Father will not forgive your sins" (NLT).

Think about the numerous times you have sinned, just today alone, from the time you opened your eyes this morning. Those are the very offenses that you will go to God and ask forgiveness for. But how do you expect to receive pardon from Him, when you are still holding on to what someone did to you? This is why the Our Father Prayer says "Forgive us our trespasses as we forgive those who trespass against us" (Matthew 6:12). This conditional request reminds us of our great dependency on God lest we become proud.

It is virtually impossible to be happy and live a fruitful life when you are tied down by bitterness and resentment. Certainly, it is better to learn how to forgive now, than to get in a marriage and allow anger to drive you apart from your husband. Practice managing your anger and choosing your words wisely. Know when and how to respond and when to bridle your tongue.

There will inevitably be times when you disagree with your future husband. But your tongue should not be reckless and your anger should not drive you to sin. Learn to walk away and think before speaking now. Learn to discuss problems without attacking a person now. Most of all learn to fight your battles on your knees in prayer now.

If your anger drives you to sin, be quick to sincerely apologize and make peace both with God and the person you have offended. Romans 12:18 says, "If possible, so far as it depends on you, live peaceably with all" (ESV). You have the responsibility to uphold peace and to bridge the gap if it has been breached between you and another person. Be courageous enough to own up to your mistakes, humble enough to apologize, and mature enough to understand the other person's perspective. Forgiveness is easier said than done, but it is also necessary.

Sometimes it can be a process of releasing the offenses and working through the repercussions of the offense. After you have released the offender, you have to allow God to take away the sting of the offense. It doesn't mean that the recollection of the offense will be wiped clean from your memory. But you will know that you have fully forgiven the person when a flashback no longer overwhelms you with anger. Forgiveness brings a sense of peace and lifts the weight of the offense from your shoulders.

Effective communication is an essential tool for dealing with offenses. We often tend to stray away from difficult conversations and many expectations go unspoken. Every incident that we harbor in anger, makes us become like a ticking bomb that can detonate at any second. Learn to communicate your needs and frustrations as soon as you are calm enough to do so and ensure that there are no misunderstandings. (I learned this one the hard way.)

Be cautious to explain why you are angry or frustrated rather than expressing that anger in an inappropriate manner. There may be some situations where you will not get closure, but you cannot allow your forgiveness to be contingent on an apology that you may never get. The most powerful thing you can do, as difficult as it may be, is to forgive a person even if they are not remorseful. In fact, you should pray that God will soften their heart, not for them to feel sorry about hurting you, but because ultimately they are offending Him. Always remember that you cannot control the actions of others and the way they feel about you. But you can control how you respond to the situation at hand. Don't allow the anger from your past to hinder you from loving people in the present.

## Prayer

Jesus, I do not want to be an angry person. I release all the offenses that have been committed against me. Please forgive me of my trespasses as I forgive those who trespassed against me. I pray that You would grant me the grace to walk in love, to be slow to anger and slow to take offense. Let the words of my mouth and the meditation of my heart be acceptable in Your sight. Amen.

# CHAPTER FOURTEEN

## *The Struggle of Strongholds*

"If the Son sets you free, you will be free indeed." John 8:36 (NIV)

*Secret Struggles: The ones that keep you up late at night*
*Balled under the blankets, trembling with fright*
*The kind that makes you cry yourself to sleep*
*That silences your voice to a whisper or a peep*
*The struggles that plague your mind and steals your sense of peace*
*That races your thoughts when you want them to cease*
*The struggle that you arrest in the depths of your heart*
*Too ashamed to speak up yet bearing its scar*

*The one you try to drink away to suppress its existence*
*Or get a temporary high to boost your resistance*
*The thing deep in your mind that eats you alive*
*The secret you fight back every day just to "survive"*
*The one that lowers your confidence and destroys your self-esteem*

*That makes you beg for a second chance and cry out to God to be redeemed*
*The struggle that makes you feel empty and plunges you into depression*
*That robs your peace of mind and stifles your progression*

*When the smoke is cleared and your high comes to a low*
*When you've run from pillar to post with nowhere else to go*
*Just know that in Christ there is still hope for you*
*That your secrets do not have to consume you*
*So, break your silence about your struggles in any shape or form*
*Because when Christ is in your crisis, you can weather any storm*

That was a poem that I wrote when I began to understand the destructive nature of secrets. They eat you alive from the inside out and take away your power. So many women walk around physically free yet mentally enslaved and fighting internal battles. We live in a '*Shh* society' where everything that we struggle with is swept under a rug as we pretend to be perfect. God forbid that someone discovered the things that make us cry at night, the battles that we fight behind closed doors, or the reason we make so many excuses to cover up the real issues. Too many single young women are secretly struggling with strongholds in the form of addictions. As this chapter goes through some common strongholds, I challenge you to dig deeper into the core issues that lead to these secret struggles and confront them head on.

## *Impulsive Spending*

If you feel compelled to buy something every time you drive by a mall or buy things out of greed instead of need, you may be an impulsive spender. The compulsion to buy something even in the absence of necessity is a poor habit. Maybe you are the type who shops online for 'therapy' to distract yourself from a bigger issue. While there is nothing wrong with treating yourself to nice things, remember the importance of saving and being a good steward of your resources.

Unhealthy spending habits affect your ability to thrive in other areas of life as well. Learn to stick to your budget so that you can meet your financial obligations. And if you don't have a budget, create one. Be prudent in your spending because it will be an important quality to have once you have financial obligations that come along with marriage.

## *Food*

Have you ever seen an episode of *My 600-lb Life* on TLC? Almost every food addiction began with a traumatic event, sometimes going as far back as childhood. They range from abandonment to the death of a loved one. Sometimes women tend to 'eat' their emotions instead of expressing them which can lead to a food addiction or disorder. Food can be considered a legal drug that we use to comfort and distract ourselves from the real issues.

If you struggle with a food addiction or an eating disorder, ask yourself what is it that you are trying to cope with or run away from. Is it because eating (or not eating) is your way of suppressing a traumatic experience? Is it your reaction to a situation? Are you depressed, dealing with disappointing news, or lost someone near to you? If so my dear, your body is merely the external shell that you have been using to cloak your internal pain. You cannot eat or starve that pain away. If you are in this predicament, then I pray that you would surrender the source of your struggles to the Lord.

I know that this is a very sensitive topic but do not be afraid to talk with someone that you trust or to seek professional assistance. Be honest about when and how your challenges with food began, the ways that your emotions and body have been impacted, and how the person can specifically support you in your journey of recovery. Be nice to yourself and be aware of your triggering emotions. Cope with those emotions using a healthy mechanism. For you that may be writing, being in the company of others, taking a nature walk, singing, or leisurely reading. Whatever your alternative, know that you are an overcomer through Christ! Keep pushing!

## *Relationships*

Are you one of those women who cannot stand being single and always need to be in a relationship? Do you rebound from one male to another without giving yourself a chance to heal? If you answered yes then you may be using relationships as space-fillers to a deeper issue like neglect, loneliness, or even low-self-esteem. Perhaps you enjoy the feeling you get when receiving good morning texts, goodnight kisses, lavish gifts, and warm hugs. Those are all beautiful things but should not be pursued as medication to a bigger problem.

Search yourself and dig deeper to the root of the issue. It is common for relationship addicts to have a past of abandonment by an important figure in their life, and later resort to overcompensating for that lost love. Maybe you have been looking for love in all the wrong persons. Many times, the new relationship does not stand a chance due to the invisible walls of mistrust that solidly enclose you. Merely going through motions, you may be searching for the comfort of the last affair by constantly comparing the new and the old guy. But I challenge you to experience the love of your heavenly Father before you jump into another relationship and see what a significant difference it makes.

# *Work*

In this modern era where women are constantly fighting for equality, they are now going head-to-head and shoulder-to-shoulder in competition for careers and positions that were once dominated by men. And while good work ethics are commendable, turning into a workaholic is not healthy and can become addictive. Being consistently busy, and not taking the time to reflect, evaluate and plan can adversely affect one's productivity.

I have a strong work ethic that can sometimes turn me into a workaholic. When I start something, I do not want to stop until it is completed. Sometimes I get so caught up that I lose track of time or forget to eat. I enjoy the rewarding feeling of accomplishing something that I have worked so hard for. But as passionate as I might be in producing good quality work, I too must check myself from time to time and ensure that I am maintaining a balance and not becoming addicted to busyness.

Busyness for us can be a concrete way to feel needed and accomplished or to avoid the feeling of loneliness. But constantly being busy does not give our lives meaning—God does. We can even become so busy doing the "work of the Lord" that we lose the heart behind it. Don't busy yourself doing heartless and meaningless work. Find the meaning in your work by engaging your heart. Pour yourself out for God's honor but don't burn yourself out in the process. Learn to keep a balance, prioritize your work, and take time for yourself.

## *Self*

Whether we would like to admit it or not, humans are driven to pursue the glory of themselves because of the wicked nature of our hearts. We are inflated with pride and make 'gods' of ourselves. Our haughty hearts long for the praises of superlative adjectives to describe our intellect, physical appearance, work ethic, and skills. We live for the approval of others and feel less valued when we are not recognized.

It is the conceited, narcissistic, and exalted view of ourselves that deceives us into believing that we are deserving of glory and honor. We take glory for our finite knowledge, fleeting possessions, vain accomplishments, and fading social status. We're addicted to the power that comes with knowledge and popularity because of the attention that it gives us. But the apostle Paul in Romans 12:3 warns us to not think of ourselves more highly than we ought to.

While there is nothing wrong with accepting compliments and recognizing our great goals in life, they should not lead us to trust our own abilities and understanding. We should not allow success, education, money, or status—which are not bad in and of themselves—to breed a sense of self-sufficiency in our hearts. All our abilities, talents, skills and knowledge should be used for the exaltation of God and not ourselves. Everything that we are and everything that we have is not because of our own strength, or because we are deserving and entitled. It is because of God's grace toward us. Without Him, our achievements mean nothing!

The gaining of earthly fortunes and the accomplishing of feats are "…worthless when compared with the infinite value of knowing Christ Jesus my Lord" Philippians 3:8 (NLT). We may be qualified by man's standards but with all our knowledge, if God is not in the picture then we would be nothing more than educated fools. First Corinthians 3:19 says "For the wisdom of this world is foolishness in God's sight" (NIV). So, let us be careful to have a sober view of ourselves.

As humans with hearts that have tendencies for haughtiness, we need to humble ourselves under the mighty hand of God and allow Him to exalt us in due time (1 Peter 5:6). Let us practice serving in silence and selflessness. Allow the glory of God to take center stage so that others may be drawn to Him and not to ourselves. All our accomplishments should echo His credit, His praise, His honor, and His glory. We are merely the vessels through which He uses to accomplish His purposes.

The Word of God serves as a mirror that shows us the ways that we have been selfish, self-righteous, conceited, and proud. Although it deflates our ego, the Word helps us to quickly realize our insufficiencies, human depravity, and the great need to be humbled by our dependence on God. We need constant reminders that everything that we have accomplished and everything that we possess comes from God. Therefore, we ought to live to make our boast in Him alone.

## *Pornography*

Yes, I said it! Pornography is an addiction that so many single young women struggle with behind closed doors, making it even more difficult to have conversations about, much less be held accountable for. Such a taboo topic hardly ever makes it into the church and many women are too ashamed to seek the help that they need. We live in an age where pornographic material is pervasive and readily accessible. Given the fact that sex is a marketing tool for the media, the problem will persist until our view of sex and the dignity of our bodies changes.

Pornography portrays women as sexual toys to be used to fulfil the lustful desires of women and men. It also creates false expectations of the sexual experience, ruins intimacy, creates trust issues, and creates unrealistic comparisons. Many times, after engaging in sexual activity the woman feels empty, used, and discarded. Pornography can be detrimental to marriages and the way that we view other people.

If you have a pornography addiction, now is the time to be set free! You first need to acknowledge that your addiction is a problem because it is displeasing to God. If you take pleasure in it, you will not want to be freed from it, because you don't see a problem with it. You must begin to see pornography the way that God does—as a distortion and perversion of the sacred sexual experience.

Although you may experience temporary euphoria, the imminent guilt that you feel is the conviction of the Holy Spirit drawing you to come back into alignment with Him. Do not continue to justify your addiction as being better than fornication, or deceive yourself into thinking that it will make you happy. Your climax can never complete you the way the God can. (Someone had to say it!)

Stop buying into the deception of the Enemy that it is a stress reliever when it adds the stress of guilt and regret in your heart. Stop blaming other people or your previous experiences for your choices to open a pornographic magazine or a website and consume its content. Admit and accept that you cannot break the addiction in your own strength because your willpower is not strong enough. You need the power of Jesus Christ to overcome.

Seek wise counsel and accountability from a trusted person who is mature in their faith and invite them to be a part of your recovery journey. Take practical and intentional steps to remove lewd materials from your home, your computer, and your cell phone. Place filters on your internet browsers and let your accountability partner create the passwords. Be prepared to flee from the temptations of sexual sin and don't give your flesh any opportunities to frolic in vain imaginations. Renew your mind in scriptures and combat the lies of the Enemy with the truth of God's Word.

Lastly, give yourself grace and know that overcoming is a process. If you happen to fall, get up and keep fighting. Do not allow the Devil to condemn you. It is in those moments that you need to run to God, not away from Him. His arms are wide open, waiting to forgive you. Come to Him with a heart of repentance—not just remorse—and you will find that God is eager to help you walk in His divine path for your life.

Even Jesus, in His perfection, was tempted by Satan. Temptation itself, however, is not a sin—giving in to temptation is. First Corinthians 10:13 says, "No temptation has taken you except what is common to man. God is faithful, who will not allow you to be tempted above what you are able, but will with the temptation also make the way of escape, that you may be able to endure it" (WEB). Thank God for His faithfulness in creating a door for us to exit out of every time we are tempted. The problem comes when we decide to not take the way of escape. We do well to remember the story of Lot's wife who turned into a pillar of salt when she looked back on the city of Sodom instead of obeying God's instruction to flee and not look back (Genesis 19:26). Sometimes we run but intentionally leave a door cracked, or revisit the very thing God is making a way of escape from.

Sometimes we consciously choose to stay in our addictions because it temporarily feels good. But we should ask ourselves "Who do I love more?" Do we love our flesh more than we love Jesus? How much does it cost to buy your compromise? A phone call? A "you up?" text message? Nothing is worth yielding to temptation!

The best way that we can overcome is by following the example of Jesus by responding to the Enemy with the Word of God. Tell him that "It is written." You will walk by the Spirit and not gratify the desires of the flesh (Galatians 5:16). Tell him that God "is able to keep you from stumbling and to present you before his glorious presence without fault and with great joy" Jude 1:24 (NIV). Tell him that you will "Get up and pray so that you will not fall into temptation" Luke 22:46 (NIV). Tell him that God gives you the victory though Christ Jesus (1 Corinthians 15:57). Tell him that you are clothed in the whole armor of God which makes you able to stand against his schemes (Ephesians 6:11). Speak the Word and use it as your weapon—your sword.

Addictions make us slaves to a deceptive master. They lead us to falsely believe that the activities we choose over God would somehow be able to satisfy us. Instead, they slowly begin to control every aspect of our lives with the result of unfulfilled expectations, and leave a void of joy and hope. The more an addiction is fed, the bigger its bottomless appetite grows. Since they can never completely satisfy needs they should all be severed from the root.

# The Strong of Strongholds

It is so important to trace the history of addictions to better understand our current conditions. Being raised in a home with a drunkard, having a parent who was a drug addict, a family history of sexual promiscuity, or a generational curse of gambling can all contribute to current challenges with addictions. Whatever the history, know that a new destiny can begin with you. You can break the cycle. Romans 6:18 says, "You have been set free from sin and have become slaves to righteousness" (NIV). Strongholds do not have to control your life, you do not have to struggle in secret, and it is never too late to overcome.

## Prayer

Jesus, I am addicted to ( insert addiction ). I recognize that I have been deceived in my thinking that it would be able to fill my void for You. Please forgive me for choosing the desires of my flesh and counter-productive space-fillers above You. I pray that You will help me to find complete satisfaction in You, as You enable me to deal with the core of my addiction. Thank You for Your grace that is enough for me, and I pray for the strength that I need to walk away from temptation. Amen.

# CHAPTER FIFTEEN

## *The Angst of Abuse*

"Praise the LORD, my soul, and forget not all his benefits—who forgives all your sins and heals all your diseases, who redeems your life from the pit and crowns you with love and compassion." Psalm 103:2-4 (NIV)

There is nothing more grievous and harrowing than to suffer at the hands of abuse in any form. The trepidation of those traumas has a significant impact on present perceptions of the world and the people around us. It distorts the lens through which current experiences are filtered and the way we interact with others. Although sometimes we try, the pain from the past cannot be stuffed into a box and shoved into the dark abyss of the subconscious. In the same manner, ongoing violations cannot be fully dismissed by activities of deflection and distraction. The invasive tentacles of abuse have a grueling way of penetrating every area of life, so it must, therefore, be confronted and not covered up.

# The Angst of Abuse

If you are suffering or once suffered abuse, please know that the quality of your life depends on how you deal with those traumatic experiences. It was not your fault but it is your fight and you do not have to continue to live as a victim. If you have been using counter-productive coping mechanisms to numb your emotions, distance or distract yourself from your experiences, then you are merely putting a bandage on a wound that needs stitches.

Ignoring these traumas is like ignoring a diagnosis of cancer. Eventually, the impact of the abuse will metastasize to every area of your life and compromise the health of your relationships, perception of self, emotional and mental stability, and your ability to function daily. Do not continue to cover it up. It's time to confront it and live a life of freedom. Don't enter marriage with your future husband as a victim but as a survivor and an overcomer.

The first and most painful thing that [you must do is accept] the reality of the abuse. You must decide that [these relationships] are unprofitable because you will carry the [baggage into your next] relationship or friendship. Allow yourself to ex[perience the emotions] of anger, fear, sadness, disappointment, and dis[gust. Allow yourself to] cry, to punch a pillow, and to give voice to that pain. Acknowledge the ways that someone has intentionally used words or actions to intimidate, threaten, demean, exploit, isolate, harm, or manipulate you in order to maintain power and control over your life. Recognize how they have been physically, sexually, economical, verbally, emotionally, or psychologically abusive to you. Recall and write down unfiltered details about how it happened, how it made you feel, how it changed your self-perception, and how you view the abuser.

> Do not run away from problems. Be comfortable w/ them knowing that you have a God that will always get you through them

Identify triggers of the trauma. Examine how it impacted your past relationships, your current life, and your present relationships.

Maybe you are haunted by flashbacks and nightmares, struggle with depression, or are constantly in a state of low self-esteem. Perhaps, previous abuses drove you to unknowingly erect walls to enclose yourself as you are not willing to trust others. Moreover, you may compound the problem by trying to drown it using adverse coping mechanisms. Maybe you experienced suicidal ideations or harm yourself. Whatever you struggle, I encourage you to identify the ways you have tried to avoid the abuse, downplay its severity, suppress the memories, make excuses for the abuser, or project your negative emotions onto others. Admit that these are just symptoms of a bigger problem. Recognize that you need the safety and support of other in order to overcome.

The second thing you need to do is share your truth. It requires a great deal of courage to talk about sensitive, painful matters but is the only way to take your power back. You may not have the words to verbalize your angst to someone else, but you've just written a comprehensive recollection of the trauma. That is a great tool to start with.

You've got to tell someone! Tell a best friend, a sister, your youth group leader, your mom, the police, your pastor—anyone you trust. Do not allow fear to stop you from getting the help you need and deserve. Seek spiritual support and professional guidance if necessary. I don't know the circumstances you are dealing with. Maybe your abuser is no longer in your life or you had to run for your

## The Angst of Abuse

life. Whatever your situation, know that you are not stuck and you don't have to suffer in silence. Tell someone! Talk about it!

After you have spoken up and invited your confidant to bear this burden with you, allow them to help you get support in taking your power back. A professional therapist can assess your situation and provide the appropriate interventions. They can help you think through practical boundaries that should be implemented and identify healthy ways to cope with your experiences. A spiritual counselor can offer prayers for complete healing and help you to understand your trauma in the context of your spiritual beliefs.

Now I know you may be wondering about how your trauma can ever be molded into a framework of spirituality. Maybe you are angry with God and do not even have the words to pray because you've hit a ceiling with Him. Perhaps you are struggling with doubt and have some questions for God. "Why did He allow tragedy in my life?" "Why didn't He intervene when I needed Him to?" "Why do bad things happen to good people?" "Is God trustworthy?" These are some difficult yet valid questions and it's okay to have them. I want to take a detour to talk in detail about the deprived state of this world and why the evil things like abuse that happen. It will help you to understand the misfortunes of life from a spiritual view and the way that you should respond.

At the genesis of time, by the words of His mouth, God spoke a perfect earth into existence—everything He created was good. He made Adam and Eve in His image and likeness to share in intimate relationship with Himself. This intimate relationship, much like our relationships today, was grounded in genuine love which was hallmarked by freewill—the ability to choose without force or restraint. God did not create robots to be in a relationship with Him; He gave us the ability to choose to love or refuse Him.

While at first Adam and Eve chose to obey God and trust that He knew what was good for them, they allowed doubt to lead to them to disobedience. They ate from the forbidden tree of the knowledge of good and evil and believed the lie that was spewed by the serpent that the fruit would make them wise like God. Adam and Eve wanted to be able to decide what was good and what was evil for themselves. They wanted to be their own 'god,' only to forfeit freedom in the Lord to become a slave to sin. This was the same reason Lucifer (Satan or the serpent) was evicted from heaven—wanting to be like God and take glory for himself (Ezekiel 28:12-19). Romans 5:12 says "When Adam sinned, sin entered the world. Adam's sin brought death, so death spread to everyone, for everyone sinned" (NLT).

Today, we still wrestle with the desire to be 'god' over our own lives, walking according to the cravings of our own flesh. Now this deprived world is characterized by the lust of the flesh (craving for physical pleasure), the lust of the eyes (craving for the things we see), and the pride of life (pride in achievements and possessions) (1 John 2:16). That means sins like uncontrolled rage, lust, drunkenness, selfishness, sexual immorality, jealousy, arrogance, and deceit lead to offenses like abuse. Yes, abuse and every other atrocity of this world are fundamentally rooted in sin.

As broken people, we were all born in sin and shaped in iniquity. That means that none of us are inherently good but are

## The Angst of Abuse

deserving of God's wrath. Our hearts are deceitful and desperately wicked (Jeremiah 7:9). It is against our very fleshly nature to do the right thing. [...] e all sinned and fallen short of God's glory (R[...] [...]allen state, we have the choice to either be a [...] ghteousness. We can choose to obey our [...] d. But that choice—freewill—does not c[...] consequences. Romans 6:23 tells us that "the [...] death, but the gift of God is eternal life in Christ Jesus o[...] d" (NIV).

[Sticky note: freewill - does not constitute freedom from consequences. Hold on to hope Romans 8:18]

Knowing that we would fall short in sin and be deserving of death, God continued to pursue us with His love by making a way to redeem us unto Himself through Christ Jesus. Jesus bore the past, present and future sins of the world so that we can have the gift of salvation—something we cannot earn on our own. This is the message of the Gospel. The greatest tragedy in the history of humanity was the death of the Son of God. But that tragedy was also the greatest triumph because through Jesus, we can be in right standing with God again. That includes murderers, liars, thieves, adulterers, fornicators, and yes, abusers too.

Our fallen state did not deter the deity of God. Rather, it proved His love and desire to be in a relationship with us despite our depravity. God is patient with all of us and desires that none of us perish but come to repentance (2 Peter 3:9). When people hurt us or we hurt others—no matter how horrific the offense—it is important to remember that the root of the offense is sin. This does not justify the offense but highlights that something is innately 'wrong' with us (sin) and that we need God who can make us right (whole) again. It highlights our need for repentance as we seek to forgive and be forgiven. We need to be delivered from evil and sometimes that means deliverance from ourselves.

Our wounds—no matter how deep and painful—should drive us toward God not away from Him. He is the only one who can save us from the wages of sin and freely give to us the gift of eternal life. "He heals the brokenhearted and binds up their wounds" Psalm 147:3 (NIV). He forgives us of our sins, heals our diseases, redeems us from the pit of death and destructions, and continuously shows us His love and compassion (Psalm 103:4).

By now you may be asking "How are we to respond to the deprived state of this world?" We are to glory in our suffering because it produces perseverance, character, and hope (Romans 5:3-4). Hope that "after you have suffered a little while [on earth], the God of all grace, who has called you to His eternal glory in Christ, will himself restore, confirm, strengthen, and establish you" 1 Peter 5:10 (ESV). Find solace in the fact that God is near to the brokenhearted (Psalm 34:18) and He will not allow your suffering to be in vain. Even though there are troubles of all sorts in this world, we can take heart because Jesus has overcome this world (John 16:33). Find hope in the promise that the "…present sufferings are not worth comparing with the glory that will be revealed in us" Romans 8:18 (NIV).

God wants to use your trauma for His glory. He wants to use it to draw you closer to Him. You may not always understand the details of why He allows some things to happen. But in the bigger picture, "…all things God works for the good of those who love him,

## The Angst of Abuse

who have been called according to his purpose" Romans 8:28 (NIV). God's thoughts and ways are far above ours (Isaiah 55:9) and we will not understand all His plans. That is what makes Him God. When our finite minds fall short, our faith extends beyond what we know and see.

I believe that God can turn your messy experiences into masterpieces. He did not allow your experiences to destroy you, but to build character, develop perseverance, stretch your faith, and to accomplish a greater purpose in your life. There is always purpose in your pain.

That was an important detour to take, but now I want to reel you back into the third step you should take in overcoming your abuse. The journey of going from the victim to the survivor of abuse requires the *F word* again—forgiveness. Forgiveness brings freedom and is therefore, a critical part of your healing process. It is the letting go of the feelings of bitterness, resentment, and anger. Forgiving someone doesn't mean that you will immediately rebuild trust with the abuser or that you are obligated to restore a relationship with them. It doesn't mean that the nature of the relationship or friendship has to be the same. It doesn't mean that the abuser will not have to face the consequences of their actions. It doesn't mean you should make excuses for the offense.

Forgiveness is a choice, not a feeling. It is a command from God, not an option. It is an expression of love and a way for you to bear the image of Christ. In the same way that God forgives us, you must be like Him and forgive others. This means that you choose to no longer to hold the offense against the person or hold a grudge in your heart. You will choose to relinquish your desire to hurt them as much as they have hurt you. You will choose to trust God enough to fight your battles—to allow vengeance to remain in His hands.

That is not an easy thing to do. But as you consciously make the decision to let go of the offense, you will find freedom. Your emotions do not have to be in control. You don't have to continue to relive the negative experiences, or live a defeated life. Forgiveness gives you your power back. It is the choice to rise again, stronger than before.

Addressing your history of abuse is imperative during your season of singleness. I cannot stress that enough! It is a huge part of your journey to wholeness. This season of your life allows you to devote quiet time with God and allow Him to heal your wounds. Be intentional about discussing the issues you have suppressed, processing unanswered questions, and speaking your truth. Now is the time to break down the emotional walls you have constructed and to talk with someone you trust. That is the path to healing. Focus on your personal growth and restoration so that the pain of your past is not projected into your future.

The struggles that you have endured and the scars that you bear are for a purpose greater than yourself. They tell the story of your survival. As you get closer to a state of wholeness, you will come to realize that everything—I mean everything—worked together for your good and God's glory. The survival of your abuse is not just for you but to help someone else to get through the same thing that you once struggled with. God does not deliver us to keep our stories a secret.

## The Angst of Abuse

There are so many other women out there who are being physically, financially, verbally, sexually, emotionally, and mentally abused. They want to escape but do not know the way out. But you've "been there and survived that" you've got to help someone else. You know what it is like to fight for your life, to be strong for your children, to cry yourself to sleep, to whisper prayers to God, and to sing songs in your heart just to keep yourself sane. You know what it is like to doubt the existence God, to question the reason bad things happen, and to feel hopeless. But you have also discovered the reality of His love despite the depravity of humanity. You would have discovered the freedom in forgiveness. You would have discovered the power in speaking your truth.

Someone, somewhere, is waiting to have their lives completely transformed by your testimony. They need to see a glimmer of hope in your story. They need to be empowered and inspired by your life's work. So, as you work through your healing process and wait on the Lord to reveal you to your future husband, get to work! Someone's life is literally depending on you.

## Prayer

Lord, my heart has been broken by abuse. I don't know how to pick up the pieces or where to begin. For so long I have run away from the truth of what has happened because it seemed easier not to deal with it. Now, Lord, I am tired of running, so I run to You. Jesus, you have already taken stripes for my emotional healing and I thank You that I am already an overcomer. Without You, I am not able to survive, so please give me the hope that I need to hold on. Thank You, Lord, for preserving my life; it reassures me that I have a purpose. Restore me to wholeness so that I may testify of Your goodness and mercy toward me. Help me to extend the same forgiveness and grace to my abuser. Thank You for being a loving God of imperfect people in a broken world. Most of all, thank You for the hope of everlasting life that is free from suffering and sin. Amen.

### Declarations of Healing and Wholeness
- In the name of Jesus, I am healed of the angst of past abuse.
- Satan has no authority or control over my mind.
- I choose to forgive my offender and release negative emotions.
- God can restore me to wholeness.

# CHAPTER SIXTEEN

## *Know Your Value*

"I praise you because I am fearfully and wonderfully made; your works are wonderful, I know that full well." Psalm 139:14 (NIV)

When was the last time you looked in the mirror and affirmed your God-given value? It's been a while, hasn't it? Let's do it right now. Declare these affirmations with me.

    I am beautiful.

    I am valuable in the sight of the Lord.

    God has a special purpose for my life.

    I am whole in Christ.

    I am both a masterpiece and a work in progress.

    Nothing happens to me that with God's help I cannot overcome!

Every time we look in the mirror these truths should stare back at us. We are reflections of the image of God because His character is revealed in His creation. His wisdom, creativity, power, and goodness are evident in the way that we were masterfully created. We have the ability to reason using our intellect, to be relational with others and to be responsible for making moral decisions. Humans are the only creatures that were made with these capacities. He designed each of us uniquely and with an innate sense of dignity. Since God is good and we were made in His likeness, it must be true that His creation is also good. We are beautiful and valuable in His eyes.

Knowing that we were created with value, beauty, dignity and purpose should determine the lives we lead and the view we have of ourselves. When you fully understand your value in Christ, you will not give discounts on your dignity, markdowns on your morals or sales on your standards. You would find yourself associating with the people and activities that contribute value to your life. You wouldn't change the person God created you to be just so others would 'like' you. You wouldn't undermine your greatness nor overcompensate to prove your worth. You would pursue your dreams without apology, cling to your beliefs without compromise, and assert your personal boundaries out of self-respect. You would simply not sell yourself short because you know your worth.

When we do not understand our value in the eyes of God, we inevitably tend to settle for less than He desires for our lives. Reflect on the times you have 'sold yourself short.' Why did you compromise your value? Think back on the times that you have stayed in toxic relationships. The times when you compromised your standards to appease someone else. The times when you gave up on a dream or passed up an opportunity. Think back to the things you did to fit in because you were too afraid to stand out. The times you were silent when you needed to speak up.

Maybe you have accepted mistreatment from men who did not value your body. Maybe you kept company with friends who pressured you to sin. Perhaps you even knew that those relationships and friendships were fruitless and futile. Nevertheless, you invested time, energy, money, and deep emotions.

Maybe you have compromised your value because you believed the lie that you are not enough—that you needed to rely on the external factors like wealth, popularity, physique, and social status to validate your innate worth. But that is a deception and the only way to dismiss deceit is by feeding yourself the truth. The truth is, your identity and value are found in Christ—not your body, your brains, or material things.

Deceit, disbelief, desperation, and disobedience can all lead you to compromise your value. It is important that you learn to see yourself as a product of God's image and not try to create an image of your own. Sometimes your own insecurities, flaws, and vulnerabilities cause you to not see yourself as God sees you. There may be times when you don't feel beautiful, strong, adequate, confident, or intelligent. But those feelings need to be brought under subjection as you develop a new way of thinking about yourself. Perhaps, you may need to start everyday with similar affirmations to those at the beginning of this chapter. But always remember that you are beautiful, you are strong and you are enough because that's the way God made you.

Remind yourself of the truths the Lord says about you. You are God's child (John 1:12), a friend of God (John 15:15), fearfully and wonderfully made (Psalm 139:14), a joint heir with Jesus (Romans 8:17), a virtuous woman (Proverbs 31:10), the temple of the Holy Spirit (1 Corinthians 6:19), and forgiven (1 John 1:9). His thoughts toward you are precious and vast in number (Psalm 139:17). His value for your life is evident by the huge price He has paid (1 Corinthians 6:20) to redeem you unto Himself through the death and resurrection of Jesus. Remind yourself of these truths. Carry yourself in a manner that reflects the value God places on you.

## Prayer

Lord, thank You for seeing the value in me, even when I sometimes do not see it in myself. Help me to not compromise that value and to not settle in unhealthy situations that threaten to detract from my dignity. Remind me constantly of the beautiful truths found in Your Word about my identity and worth in You. Amen.

# CHAPTER SEVENTEEN

## *Guarding Your Heart*

"Above all else, guard your heart, for everything you do flows from it." Proverbs 4:23 (NIV)

If you are a dog lover like I am, you probably find yourself in the veterinarian's office a few times per year purchasing Heart Gard chewable tablets. The beef-flavored tablets protect pets against heartworms, roundworms, and hookworms. Just as we take measures to protect our pets against these parasites, we also should protect ourselves from anything that tries to take up wrongful residence in our hearts.

Guarding your heart is not just about setting up personal boundaries to restrict sexual intimacy outside of marriage. It is more about protecting your mind, your emotions, and your desires. These are the components of your heart. They make up who you are, help to shape your character, and determine everything that you do.

If you want to pursue the things of Christ, then you should align your heart with His heart. In order to follow the heart of God, you have to be in an intimate relationship with Him. Without constantly chasing God, you will end up chasing the evil desires of your own heart. That is why you ought to cautiously protect your thoughts, emotions, intentions, dreams, ambitions and desires from *parasites* like youthful lusts, pride, enviousness, gossip, slander, complaining, jealousy, sexual immorality, unforgiveness, bitterness, and any other sin that does not conform to the image Christ.

Sin is the result of a toxic combination of desire and opportunity for the things that are not of Christ. Therefore, guarding your heart against sin should take a dual approach—the internal conforming of your desires to God's desires, and the external application of wisdom to resist opportunities (temptation) to sin. The first thing you should do is pray. Pray for the strength to flee temptation and to resist the sins that try to destroy your heart. Pray that God would conform your desires to His. Pray for the guidance of the Holy Spirit and conviction that leads to swift repentance. Prayer keeps you connected to the heart of God and dependent on Him in all your ways. Intimacy with God will drive you to pursue His desires over your own; to be led by His wisdom and not your emotions.

After you have prayed, it's time to apply practical wisdom. "The fear of the Lord is the beginning of wisdom…" Proverbs 9:10 (NIV). That fear is your reverence of God that brings you to a state of awe because of His goodness, sovereignty and beauty. It will create an awareness that He desires holiness and your obedience to His

## Guarding Your Heart

Word. This fear of God produces wisdom which helps you walk daily in a way that reflects your love and reverence for Him.

Practically speaking, it is wise to guard your heart by putting measures in place that protect it from the sins that easily ensnare and take your eyes off God. That means work—every day you are called to crucify the flesh and its desires. The way to die to the sinful desires of your heart is by being intentional about feeding your spirit the Word of God. Constantly rely on the power of God to keep you from yielding to the temptation of engaging in any form of sin. Be aware of the slightest potential to sin and allow your love for God to drive you to do everything in your power to resist that temptation. Be aware about what you open your eyes, ears and mouth to as they are all gateways to the heart and mind. "Fix your thoughts on what is true, and honorable, and right, and pure, and lovely, and admirable. Think about things that are excellent and worthy of praise" Philippians 4:8 (NLT). That is the way to guard your heart against sin.

Guarding your heart against non-beneficial connections with others is something that requires spiritual discernment. Overtime, you will realize that every acquaintance is not an ally. Every buddy is not a best friend. Every male it not a mate. Only wisdom can show you the difference.

It is your responsibility to pray about the connections you allow in your life. Whenever a male expresses romantic interest toward you and the feelings are mutual, prayerfully and continuously take those desires to the Lord and ensure that they are in alignment with His will. Your reverence for God and desire to please Him will not allow you to be comfortably connected with anyone or anything outside of His will. Talking to God can save you so much time and discomfort because He gives you His wisdom in guarding your heart.

Prayer will help you to spiritually discern qualities about a man long before you become emotionally invested deeply. That is why you need to seek God first. When God shows you that your connection with that male is in His will, gradually the relationship becomes a safe space to reveal more about yourself. You will become more comfortable in slowly taking down the guards down and opening your heart completely. The same is true of platonic friendships.

This was something that I struggled to understand for a long time. I thought guarding my heart meant that I should keep my walls up so high that it would be difficult for anyone to connect with me. I would block people out and deny the potential of fruitful friendships and relationships because I feared being hurt. I had trust issues and I did not want to be emotionally vulnerable with anyone. I feared allowing people to get to know me intimately, and as soon as anyone got close to me, I pulled away.

Now I understand the importance of spiritually discerning my relationships. I allow those who are willing to protect the treasures of my heart to walk with me as we together pursue of the will of God's heart. Mutual trust and vulnerability in these relationships require the prayerful removal of the guards. That level of intimacy is built on trust and a love that dispels the fears of rejection, failure and being hurt.

Deep connectivity and accountability with the people we trust come through vulnerability. Sometimes as single women we keep our barriers up all the time and portray ourselves as a strong and independent. But we have to be careful to not be so guarded that we forfeit all possibilities of connectivity, even on a friendship or mentorship level. Don't be afraid to keep it real with those you trust. Your realness makes you relatable. It's okay to share your life with others and allow them to see the authentic you. That is the only way others can walk with you through the difficult seasons of life, encourage you in the things of God, correct you when you are wrong, and be supportive of your dreams.

Don't be so guarded that you do not accept help when it is sincerely being offered. Don't be too proud to ask for help when you need it. Learn to accept a compliment and allow men to be gentlemen. Don't automatically assume that every male who holds the door for you is trying to get your number. Give others the opportunity to show themselves as trustworthy. Your openness (using prayerful discernment) and friendliness will help you to build healthy bonds with others and will prepare you for being vulnerable and intimate with your future husband.

Being too guarded can minimize your interactions with others to superficial conversations. If all your conversations are small talk, then you are probably failing to chat about the things that matter. The truth is, we are all struggling with something and we all need to be encouraged in those areas. You may have survived the same grief, addictions, illnesses, or financial struggles as someone else. Those are points of connectivity and avenues to help and to be helped by others. They may need to hear your story so that they have hope to cling to.

Don't be so guarded because of fear, that you pass up the opportunity to intimately connect with others. Engage your heart, not just romantically, but also in real life issues like social injustice, poverty, hunger, or homelessness. These are the types of issues that you cannot make an impact on if you do not passionately engage your heart.

Guarding your hearts does not mean putting up a wall as a defense mechanism to block yourself from connecting with others. (That may cause you to unknowingly push away your future husband). It is having the authenticity and vulnerability to love others by prayerfully engaging ourselves, while pursuing the heart of God.

## Prayer

Lord, I understand that guarding my heart means conforming my desires to Yours and being cautious to not allow my heart to engage in the things that are not of You. I know that everything I do flows from my heart—my will, thoughts, emotions and desires. Help me to spiritually discern my relationships as I stay intimately and prayerfully connected to You. Help me to not push people away because of fear, but to lovingly embrace them so that I can meaningfully engage with them. Amen.

# CHAPTER EIGHTEEN

## *Draw the Line, and Don't Cross It*

"Let your yes mean yes, and your no mean no. Anything more than this comes from the evil one." Matthew 5:37 (CEB)

When you were a child and you asked your mom to buy you a candy bar at the checkout counter and she told you "no," you dared not to ask her again. It was because her no meant no, and she was not prepared to change her stance. While you thought she was depriving you of that sweet treat, she knew that it would spoil your appetite, or worse, rot your teeth. Your mom made a judgment call based on what she thought was best for your well-being. So, she enforced boundaries on how much candy you could eat and did not compromise her decision. Boundaries in your relationships with others should work the same way. Your "no" should mean no and your "yes" should mean yes. Whenever you begin to compromise, gray area is created and the lines become blurred.

Boundaries are essential to establish because they protect your priorities, time, energy, values, peace of mind and self-worth. It is a part of taking care of yourself because you teach people how to treat you based on what you accept. If you don't set clear boundaries, you will be violated because others have not been 'taught' how to respect you. Your boundaries are reflections of your self-respect and should not be compromised. Anyone who truly loves you will respect you enough not to cross the lines that you have drawn.

Conversations about boundaries are not always comfortable but they are always necessary. Learn to be forthright in unapologetically setting your limits without feeling the need to give long explanations about why you deserve to be respected. Be polite yet firm. Say "no" without feeling guilty. Say "yes" without feeling obligation. Be courageous enough to have tough conversations instead of blindly agreeing or suppressing your feelings just to avoid confrontation.

As a wife in waiting, one of the first boundaries you need to establish is your unavailability to married men and men who are already in a relationship. God is not the author of confusion and He will not send you someone else's husband or boyfriend. You are not a third wheel, a side chick, or an afterthought! Marital vows are a serious commitment to God, and any man who is not willing to forsake all others will probably forsake you too.

The second boundary you should seek to establish is taking premarital sex off the table in any relationship. As you have already read, sex by God's design is more than a physical activity but the knitting together of two married souls. Engaging in sexual intercourse outside of that context can cloud your judgement and distort your ability to discern a person for who they really are. A man who truly respects you will have enough integrity to guard your sexual purity and push you to honor God in that way. When you make that boundary clear, the motive of your partner's heart will be revealed. If he is serious about leading you in sexual purity, he will join you in establishing precautionary measures to avoid crossing that line.

Through the lens of fornication, you will not be able to see red flags about a person's character because of the strong appetite for sexual intimacy. Close friends and family members may try to warn you about potential danger but you won't be able to recognize it if you are unlawfully tied to the person in question. The purpose of setting this boundary is not only to obey God, but to allow yourself to discern the motives, desires, ambitions, and character of a man before going down the aisle to meet him. By abstaining from premarital sex, you are not depriving yourself, but protecting yourself from the dangers of a weakened discernment.

A third boundary that you need to establish has to do with the content of your conversations. I have learned that conversational compromise come through doors that were intentionally left open. Sometimes we fail to be assertive about topics that should not be up for discussion and later find ourselves meandering in vain imaginations, mental fantasies, and flirtatious exchanges. As single women, there are just some topics that should not surface in our conversations, some questions that are better left unanswered, some things that are better left unexplored. We don't need to start thinking about baby names after a second date. We don't need to share sexual fantasies or deeply intimate thoughts. The door to these conversations should only be opened to our husbands. Our thoughts and words are like trains that need to be guided by tracks in order to be steered in the right direction. Without such guidance, we can find ourselves in conflict, in compromise or in both.

God's Word serves as a guide for our conversations. Ephesians 4:29 tells us "Let no corrupting talk come out of your mouths, but only such as is good for building up, as fits the occasion, that it may give grace to those who hear (ESV). If there would be no benefit or encouragement if others heard our conversations publicly, then exchange of words should probably not be said privately. When the things that are honorable, true, pure, lovely, admirable and excellent permeate our thoughts, they then will show up in our conversations.

The content of our conversations should not only be guided over the telephone or during face-to-face interactions but also in our text messages and direct messages. What's going down in your DM (direct message)? What are you saying in those late-night texts? Your conversations should have no traces of eggplant and peach emojis. The next time you get a "wyd" (what you doing) text at 11pm, I hope you say "praying and going to sleep." The next time you get a "come over" text at 1am, I hope you hit the 'delete contact' button. The next time you get the "Netflix and chill" (casual way to ask for sex) message, I hope you hit the 'block' button. Please realize that chances are these men do not have boundaries for themselves and do not respect your boundaries either. Don't allow late night emotions to override your intelligence. Keep your conversations wholesome.

The fourth boundary of physical touch is the one that always seems to get convoluted, when in fact, it is not that complicated. The looming question seems to be "How far is too far?" Cuddling? Kissing? It is apparent to me that the real question is "How far can we go before it is considered sin?" I will allow you to determine the answer to that question for yourself. If God tells us to pursue holiness and to flee sexual immorality, it means that our aim should be to walk away from the line of sexual sin, not try to see how close we can get to it without crossing it. Our desire to please Him should drive us as far away as possible from anything that has even the slightest potential to displease Him.

Given your knowledge of your own weaknesses and level of discipline, ask yourself whether it is wise to engage in any activity that can potentially lead you to fall into sin. Ask yourself whether that activity helps to build you up spiritually or takes your mind to a place that is far from God. If the answer is "Yes, I would be mentally or physically driven away from God," then do not engage. It's that simple!

Don't knowingly put yourself in situations that can lead you to compromise your boundaries. Don't keep the company of people who will lead you to sin. Do your best (with the help of the Holy Spirit) to walk away from the lines and not stand on them or cross over them. Whenever your boundaries are tested—because they will be—you must be ready to uphold them. Always be ready to discern temptation, to apply wisdom, to lean on the strength of God, to resist Satan at first sight, to expose his lies using scripture, and to submit to God's will.

Boundaries do not just apply to our relations with others but also to ourselves. Your personal convictions give you wisdom in the decisions you make, the activities you engage in, the content you consume through your eyes and ears, or the places you go. Setting boundaries for yourself is a great way to develop discipline and mature in your faith. For you, that may mean limiting how much time you spend on social media, avoiding certain television shows, or not listening to a specific genre of music. If these things have even the potential to lead you to sin, then it is wise to avoid them at all cost.

My aim is not to impose my personal convictions as a legalistic normative, nor to encourage libertinism. You can establish your own boundaries using the knowledge of your weaknesses, the convictions of your heart, the Word of God, and the guidance of the Holy Spirit. The Bible may not directly speak to every situation we are faced with, but it does offer principles of wisdom. Avoid the things that disturb your conscience. Be resolve and "…make up your mind not to put any stumbling block or obstacle in the way of a brother or sister" Romans 14:13 (NIV) by parading in your freedom in the areas of their weakness. Lastly, "…make every effort to do what leads to peace and to mutual edification" Romans 14:17 (NIV). Use such principles in setting your boundaries and don't cross those lines!

## **Prayer**

Lord, please give me the wisdom that I need to set healthy boundaries and the strength to uphold them. Help me to respect myself and my boundaries enough to be immovable in my "yes" or "no." I need You to help me tame my thoughts so that my conversations and actions are honorable. Sometimes it is tempting to cross boundaries out of curiosity but help me to believe that Your way is better for me. Please help me to exercise self-discipline in all things. Amen.

# CHAPTER NINETEEN

## *A Stand for Purity*

"Flee from sexual immorality. All other sins a person commits are outside the body, but whoever sins sexually, sins against their own body." 1 Corinthians 6:18 (NIV)

When we look at the world, it is not very difficult to see how the moral compass of society is rapidly disintegrating before our very eyes. The things that were once considered abominable have become more acceptable. The pursuit of pleasure has become like chasing the wind—the more we get, the emptier we feel. Censorship makes little sense when curse 'bombs' and images of half-naked bodies make regular appearances on our television screens. They are justified as free speech and freedom of expression. Promiscuity, homosexuality, pornography, adultery, and teenage pregnancy are all just a touch of a button away—and we call it entertainment. Our tolerance level for sexual immorality has heightened as we have become desensitized to the things that once made us cringe in disapproval.

Children are being exposed to lewd material prematurely through music, books, cell phones, and the internet. As long as technology continues to evolve, peer pressure persists, and media industries continue to profit from feeding our minds poison, the problem of sexual immorality will not go away anytime soon. In fact, it is becoming more and more difficult to live in purity in an impure world. The pursuit of pleasure is robbing us of the precious gift of purity.

The concept of sexual purity has been minimized in definition to the absence of premarital sex. In the eyes of God, however, purity entails so much more than just virginity or celibacy. Long before the activities of sexual immorality manifest, impure and unguided thoughts were conceived. That is where sexual impurity begins—in the mind and heart.

Vain imaginations are the breeding ground for lustful thoughts and desires. Even though man looks at the outward appearance, God looks at the heart (1 Samuel 16:7) and holds us accountable to a standard of purity. God wants us to flee from all forms of sexual immorality, not flirt with it or frolic in it whether overtly or covertly. He calls us to be holy as He is holy (1 Peter 1:16).

Sexual sins among single young women are often secret struggles and anything that is kept in secret is more complicated to confront. This issue is particularly compounded when sex is still a taboo topic in some churches. Instead of being proactive in offering guidance and practical wisdom for living sexually pure, some churches are reactive to the repercussions of sexual immorality.

Perhaps, more private counselling sessions are held to rectify the consequences of sexual sin, than transparent teachings and sobering sermons on its dangers are delivered. This is also an issue if the church is supposed to serve as a moral compass for world. Its silence or compliance can be lethal.

A part of fleeing sexual immorality requires us to boldly say "NO" in the face of temptation while depending on God for the strength to overcome (1 Corinthians 10:13). He promises to make a way of escape and not to leave us defenseless. But we must choose to take that way out and run—literally if necessary! We cannot play around with sexual sin because sexual sin surely isn't playing around with us. It wants to destroy our relationships, tarnish our character, pervert our minds, wreck our lives, and jeopardize our eternity.

Satan is crafty in the way that he glamorizes sexual immorality to distract us from pursuing purity. He wants to make us feel like we are missing out on the time of our lives, only to leave us with memories of the biggest regrets of our lives. He will try to make sexual immorality appear to be innocent and harmless so that we can let our guards down and let sin 'slide.' But I'm sure you've heard that saying "Everything that glitters isn't gold." Some things are just gold-plated.

The lies of Satan are glamorized garbage. A bite into sexual sin may be temporarily tasty, but the consequences are bitter because sin separates us from God. Just ask Adam and Eve. That is why we have been called to "put on the Lord Jesus Christ, and make no provision for the flesh, to gratify its desires" Romans 13:14 (ESV).

"The mind governed by the flesh is death, but the mind governed by the Spirit is life and peace" Romans 8:6 (NIV).

God has created us as sexual beings. Sex in and of itself is not sinful; in fact, God created it to be enjoyable. But when we engage in any form of sex outside of the intended context of marriage, we taint something God created to be pure. If we want to maintain the purity of something beautiful, then we must take practical precautions to flee tempting situations, cast down vain thoughts, and surrender idle desires that try to compromise the sanctity of sex. We cannot put our trust in our own ability to endure sexual temptation because we will surely fail. We are not invincible to play with the 'fire' of sexual immorality and not get burned.

Sex outside of its intended context is not really a pleasure if it comes with guilt. Hence, the oxymoron "guilty pleasure." In the times that we are temporarily satisfied, we deceive ourselves into believing that the bitterness of sexual sin is "sweet." The "live a little" excuse gets carelessly tossed around as selfish desires are gratified and God's will is disregarded. When we feed our flesh and starve our spirit, the flesh becomes stronger as our spirit becomes weak. Soon the voice of God and the convictions of the Holy Spirit are quieted to a whisper.

When we find 'comfort' in sexual sin, the potency of our convictions becomes weakened. We run the risk of our minds becoming reprobated and God giving us over to our sinful ways (Roman 1:28). This is why we should flee, not flirt with sexual sin. It always takes us further than we want to go, keeps us longer than we intended to stay, and costs more than we intended to pay.

"How can a young man [or woman] keep [his or her] way pure? By guarding it according to your Word" (Psalm 119:9 ESV). The Word of God is the best weapon you have to defeat sexual impurity. But dot just learn scriptures, apply it! Merely knowing Scripture without practical application is like being defeated in battle because you refused to use your weapon.

You have to always be willing and ready to fervently fight against sexual impurity, particularly in a world that constantly confronts us with immorality. Find ways to continuously renew your mind. Here are a few suggestions. Write sticky notes and post them around the house to remind yourself of your stand for purity. Write scriptures on your mirrors or set them as your screensavers. Install filters and pop-up blockers on your Internet. "…Take captive every thought to make it obedient to Christ" 2 Corinthians 10:5 (NIV).

If you are the type of woman who needs accountability, find a prayer partner and talk to someone you trust. Choose someone who will not pacify you in the sin, but will push you to do better, and pray with and for you. James 5:16 (NLT) says, "Confess your sins to each other and pray for each other so that you may be healed. The earnest prayer of a righteous person has great power and produces wonderful results." Confession helps you to find liberty when you speak your truth. In doing so, sin loses its power and God is glorified.

The most important thing to remember is that we engage in sin (sexual or non-sexual) whenever our hearts are not completely content in God. Maintaining sexual purity requires us to love God more than we love our fleshly desires. If we love Him, we will keep is commandments (John 14:15). I challenge you to trust that God's way is better even if it doesn't always feel that way.

Even though purity seems to be blatantly disregarded in this era, it is still something that God takes seriously. It doesn't matter if people change or pop culture changes because God's standard doesn't change, neither will His Word. God's way may be deemed antiquated by the world, but it is always relevant and right.

Since God's way is always right and our desires are sometimes tainted, we have to be cautious in our curiosities. Not every desire that we have needs to be acted on. Not every feeling needs to be acted on. Feelings and emotions are fickle and if we are led solely by them, they can potentially leave us 'spiritually crippled.' This is not to say that we should ignore the fact that we are sexual beings with sexual desires. That is the way God created us. However, the expression of those desires must not be perverted to temporarily gratify our flesh.

Take a stand against sexual impurity. "Put to death, therefore, whatever belongs to your earthly nature: sexual immorality, impurity, lust, evil desires and greed, which is idolatry" Colossians 3:5 (NIV). Every day, you have to live with the determination to die to your flesh and present your body as a living sacrifice that is holy and acceptable unto the Lord.

The only way that we can rightfully express our sexual desires and live a life of purity is to view God through the right lens. God created us with those desires and His instructions for us is to wait to express them in His intended context. His intentions are not to harm us or stop us from experiencing the good things in life. As a loving

Father, He not only gave us instructions to wait, but He also gives us the Holy Spirit who empowers us to be obedient. He is not asking us to do the impossible.

We have to love God more than we love our flesh and desire to please Him more than we desire to please ourselves. Sex was designed to be pleasurable and if you have already had that experience, you may find it hard to give up something that feels good. But even something that feels good can be bad for us if it is done in the wrong context. I challenge you to believe that God's purpose for sex in marriage is better and more rewarding than your desire for sex outside of marriage. Ask for God's forgiveness, and take a stand for purity today. When you turn your affections to God, know that He is faithful to keep you in your journey of purity.

## Prayer

Lord, You desire for me to be holy as You are holy. In this overly-sexualized society it is so challenging to remain pure. Help me to live by Your standards and not the standards of this world. I want to use Your Word as a weapon to defeat sexual impurity. Help me to view You as a loving Father who wants the best for me. Thank You for giving me the strength that I need to overcome sexual impurity. Lord, I ask that You please renew my mind and purify my heart daily. Amen.

# CHAPTER TWENTY

## *"That Guy"*

"Do not give dogs what is sacred; do not throw your pearls to pigs. If you do, they may trample them under their feet, and turn and tear you to pieces." Matthew 7:6 (NIV)

To some, he may be *Prince Charming*, but all he has is charm but no royalty. He flirts with every woman he comes across so he has no loyalty either. His weekends are spent in the company of weak friends. His greatest goal is to climb success ladders instead of climbing in spiritual maturity. His most coveted possession is his car and he is driven by the pursuit of money. His childish mind is trapped in a man's body. Though he may not be short in stature, he is short in vision. He has no sense of purpose because his identity is built in vanity. Instead of making an effort, he makes excuses. He avoids serious conversations and cannot handle conflict maturely. He is emotionally unavailable and is afraid of commitment. He is just not ready to settle down, yet he expects you to *settle* for him. *That* guy!

If you've met someone similar to that description, run! Don't settle. Don't waste your time idly waiting for him to grow up. Don't try to change him into the person you want him to be. Don't overcompensate in order for him to see your value. Just run sis!

I have seen so many women settle in relationships with men who are halfway committed and all-the-way immature. They go through more stress trying to maintain the relationship than not being in it at all. Women in these types of relationships are loyal yet lonely. Dedicated yet disappointed. They spend so much time trying to do a job that only God can do—change his heart.

A man cannot be threatened, manipulated, nagged, or tricked into being mature and living in biblical manhood. You can't force him to love you by having sex with him. You can't cook and clean your way into gaining his commitment. He has to want change for himself. That change and maturity may take months or even years.

My sister, please hear me when I say that you cannot change the heart of a man. Think about how hard it is to change yourself! No matter how good of a woman you are, you would never be 'good enough' for a man that is not ready to grow up. Yes, that means missionary dating (dating a person for the purpose of converting them to Christianity) is also not acceptable. A relationship cannot be sustainable if you are unequally yoked with a man. Your concealed motive to 'convert' him just so you can be a couple is an unstable foundation to build on. If, by chance, he does convert through coercion, you will be back at square one when he reverts by choice. That's because his conversion was based on your harassment, not his heart change. Bringing him to church does not transform his heart if he only came to stop you from nagging him.

If you both disagree on your core values, you will put yourself at risk of compromising your convictions. Instead of being a stepping stone in your faith, he will become a stumbling block. Your future husband will lead you to the things of Christ, and not wait around to have you lead him. His heart is after God and he will join you in your pursuit of Him. So yes, he may be cute, but does he love Jesus? He may have charisma but is he saved? He may have a great career but can he pray? He may be intellectual but does he know the Word? He may follow the latest trends but does he follow God? If the answer is no, then what exactly are you waiting for?

The only thing you can do for a man who is an unbeliever is pray—not for him to commit to you but for him to commit to God. A man who is not committed to God certainly won't be able to commit to you. The salvation of his soul is for more important than your desire to be with him. You should not be unequally yoked with unbelievers because righteousness and wickedness have nothing in common (2 Corinthians 6:14). You cannot walk together with someone unless you are in agreement with them.

Your future husband will walk into your life prepared to take the lead and ready to commit. He will not play games with your emotions nor be inconsistent in his pursuit of you. His leadership ability will remind you of Moses. His praise to God will remind you of David. His endurance will remind you of Job. His passion for the kingdom will remind you of Paul. His strength will remind you of Samson. His faith will remind you of Abraham. His courage will remind you of Daniel. His wisdom will remind you of Solomon. And his love will remind you of Jesus. Wait for the Lord to reveal you to *that* guy!

## Prayer

Lord, thank You for creating me as a treasure. Help me to cherish and value myself the way that You cherish and value me. I am willing to wait on Your perfect timing and not settle for a man who is not committed to You. Lord, please continue to prepare me to be a blessing to my future husband, because I know that he will be a blessing to me. Amen

# CHAPTER TWENTY-ONE

## *Mission of Maturity*

"When I was a child, I talked like a child, I thought like a child, I reasoned like a child. When I became a man, I put the ways of childhood behind me." 1 Corinthians 13:11 (NIV)

When you were a child, you probably enjoyed games like hopscotch and jump rope. Those games were age-appropriate, but when you became a teenager, your interests started to shift. Maybe you were less into riding bicycles and more into books. When you became an adult, you probably were more interested in putting into practice what you read in your books on how to start a business or how to write a grant proposal. As the stages of life changed, so did you. And as you matured, you put away more of your old childish ways.

*Adulting* requires us to assume responsibilities like working a full-time job, paying rent, a mortgage, or car note, or making our own decisions. But maturity is more than just meeting financial obligations and having autonomy. Maturity is being able to prioritize responsibilities, sacrifice for long-term benefits, and develop new interests. It is the ability to interact respectfully with others, articulate thought effectively, control emotions, and ask questions with a yearning for understanding. Maturity is being able to accept constructive criticism, give helpful feedback, think critically and independently, and accept personal responsibility for shortcomings. It is setting long-term goals, learning life lessons, applying wisdom to all situations, and committing to continued spiritual, personal, and professional development.

Maturity is never accomplished in comfort zones. In life, we sometimes go through uncomfortable seasons that stretch our faith, challenge our limits, force us to confront our fears, and push us to embrace new experiences. As 21$^{st}$ century women, one of our greatest qualities can also become one of our greatest setbacks. Some of us have become so strong and 'independent' that we push away the support, wisdom, and guidance of others.

I know that the difficulties of life may have put you into survival mode. Maybe you had to raise a child on our own or bear the responsibility of paying bills at a very young age. Maybe you didn't have all of the opportunities you needed to be successful. Maybe you learned to change your own tires and unclog your own drains. Perhaps you've worked hard to be able to take on the same jobs as men, hold down your own household, and provide for yourself and your children.

Those experiences may have driven you to learn to survive on our own and it is absolutely amazing that you are still standing strong. But you do not have to be strong on your own. A part of maturing is laying aside your pride and allowing the people God placed in your life to walk alongside you and help carry your burdens (Galatians 6:2). One day He will send your husband to walk with you and help shoulder some of that load. You may not need him to pay your bills, but you might need him to fix the three cars in your garage. You might not need him to buy the food in your house, but he may be a better chef than you. You might not need him to earn more money, but you might need his help in budgeting and management.

It takes maturity to allow someone else to become intimately involved in your world to help you. We were not created for independence and isolation. We were created to exist in interdependent communities and companionships. I hope that as you mature, you will learn to let go of the need to always be in control and allow others to journey with you.

As a wife in waiting, you may be wondering which immature ways and childish things you should be putting away. Well, I've got quite the list. It is time to put away gossiping, slander, and envy. Let go of self-righteousness and shortsightedness, insubordination to authority and imprudence in decisions. It's time to let go of pride, misaligned priorities, and poor communication. Put away laziness and idleness, vain conceit and selfish ambitions. Lay aside immodestly and insecurity, uncleanliness and ungodliness. If any of these qualities characterize you, invite someone to walk alongside you to hold you accountable and to challenge you to mature gracefully.

As you grow older, you may start to notice your life goals changing, your conversations becoming weightier, your confidence level rising, and the way you handle adversity improving. Maybe you will apologize sooner when you offend someone, have greater patience and self-control, and handle your anger better. These changes are all evidence that you are maturing and you should challenge yourself to continue growing in other areas as well.

You are on a lifelong journey of learning from your mistakes, gleaning from the experiences of others, solving problems, asking questions, taking on challenges, and inspiring change. Continue to make your dreams a reality, sacrifice for the sake of others, leave your footprints in the sand of history, and commit to your passions. Most of all, become the person you were created to be and live for a purpose greater than yourself.

Become self-aware, teachable, and well-rounded. Have intellectually stimulating conversations that challenge you to think deeply, contemplate your worldviews, and solidify your values and beliefs. Use your time to foster wifely and motherly qualities. Develop well-defined goals then surrender them to God for His stamp of approval. Take calculated risks, acknowledge when you have made mistakes and seek to not make them again. Speak the truth in love and encourage other women. Be open to constructive criticism, stop punishing yourself for your past, and continuously strive to become better.

Respect yourself, take care of your health, and do everything in the spirit of excellence. Keep your heart filled with gratitude and humility, and your arms outstretched in service without expecting anything in return. Let your spirit be humble and gentle, your prayers powerful, and your advice wise. Know when to speak and when to remain silent. Work for what you want and depend on God to provide your needs. Don't pretend to be perfect but rather allow

God's strength to be made perfect in your weakness. Seek community with other believers who help to nurture your walk with Christ. Inspire others with your testimony and let your beautiful feet carry the gospel.

Speaking of the gospel, there are few things that are more dangerous than spiritual immaturity. The day you accepted Christ should have been the commencement of a new journey with Him. Your walk with God should not have become stagnant after a few months of professing your faith or saying a prayer for salvation. You should be steadily progressing and maturing.

Your knowledge, experiences, and encounters with God should not be the same as when you first got saved. Spiritual fruits and gifts should be the evidence of your maturity. Your reservoir of scriptures should go beyond John 3:16, and your understanding of salvation should be more than a 'get-out-of-hell-free' card. Your discernment should be sharp enough to identify false prophets and embellished teachings. Your knowledge of God should go beyond the simplified and condensed 45-minute Sunday School lessons.

There should be a difference in your lifestyle after you got saved. You should not still be carnal-minded, stumbling over the same snares from five years ago, and falling prey to the same tricks of the Enemy time after time. You should not still be praying heartless and rehearsed 30-second prayers before bed and solely depending on others to feed you God's Word. These are all signs of spiritual immaturity.

As single Godly women, we should be spending time maturing in the things of Christ and becoming more like Him. If we want Godly men, then we also need to be spiritually mature. Our future husbands will need women who can wage war in prayer against the schemes of the Enemy, who can teach their children the way of the Lord, and who can digest spiritual meat with him.

Although we will never reach a plateau of knowing all that there is to know about Christ we should continuously be reaching for higher heights and deeper depths in Him. Never become stagnant and content with your understanding and relationship with God. Your relationship with the Lord is the foundation of every other relationship in your life. The more time you spend with Him, the more you will notice maturity in every other area of your life, and the more familiar you will become with His voice.

During your season of being single, begin your lifelong mission of maturing and becoming whole in every area of your life. Remember that growth does not come in comfort zones. If you want to mature you must be willing to take on a challenge and invite people to walk with you through that process. Don't limit your challenges; challenge your limits.

## Prayer

Lord, please show me the areas of my life where I still need to 'grow up.' Help me to put away my childish ways as I seek to be more like You. I don't just want to be an adult, but a Godly woman who is mentally, emotionally, spiritually, socially, personally, and professionally matured. Remind me that maturing is a lifelong mission that requires me to take on new challenges and invite others to share in that journey. Amen.

# CHAPTER TWENTY-TWO

## *Wife Material*

"He who finds a wife finds a good thing and obtains favor from the LORD." Proverbs 18:22 (ESV)

"The Lord God said, 'It is not good for the man to be alone. I will make a helper suitable for him'" Genesis 2:18 (NIV). Since the genesis of time, God has created us for companionship. It is not suitable to our nature to be isolated or completely independent. Being in close relationship with others helps to maximize the purpose for which we were created. We find completion in Christ and community in each other. Unity empowers husbands and wives to draw on the strengths of each other to accomplish that which God has set out for them to do. This is why Ecclesiastes 4:9-10 says "Two are better than one, because they have a good return for their labor. If either of them falls down, one can help the other up" (NIV). The two are dependent on each other for support, encouragement, prayers, intimacy, and love. Life's trials become easier to bear and triumphs become merrier to share when we have someone walking alongside us—someone of the same nature and likeness who is able to relate to us. God designed the man and the woman to be interdependent because He knew that there is only so much we can do, or so far we can go on our own.

When God saw Adam in the garden alone He saw the need for the man to have a helper. He then made Eve, who was taken from Adam's rib to walk alongside him and to support him. If God saw that the man needed a wife, then it must mean that she possessed the qualities that would pull out the best in him. I want to discuss some of these qualities to help us prepare for becoming helpers to our husbands.

## *Effective Communicator*

One of the ways that you can be a blessing to your future husband is by respecting him with your words. Words have the power to build up or tear down; encourage or discourage; help or hurt. As a helpmeet, your words are supposed to be truthful and spoken in love (Ephesian 4:25). Use them to support, comfort, and encourage. When his business plan falls through, tell him to try again. When he feels weak, remind him of his strength in Christ. Tell him how wise he is and how much you love him. "Gracious words are a honeycomb, sweet to the soul and healing to the bones" Proverbs 16:24 (NIV). Being able to use your words to effectively communicate your thoughts, concerns, desires, and emotions is pertinent in any relationship, particularly marriage.

You can practice your communication skills with your friends and family now. Try to go a little bit further than the typical "Hello, how are you" line. Talk about things that matter; things that are of a lasting impact. It will help you to articulate your thoughts and feelings, and formulate your opinions. Practice listening keenly not only to responding but also to relate. Learn to actively listen without interrupting and give eye contact. It shows that you are interested and fully engaged. Ask questions instead of making assumptions.

In the times when there are differences in opinions, seek to understand the perspective of the communicator instead of rigidly defending your own position. In times of disagreement, both parties should walk away with at least the feeling that they were heard and understood. Don't allow differences in opinions to drive wedges in your relationships. Instead of fighting with mean words, learn to fight on your knees. Pray for unity through misunderstandings and direction in disagreements.

## *Prayer Warrior*

Communicating with God is just as important as communicating with others. Prayers should be the most important conversations of your day. The beauty about praying is that there is no special time or place in which to do it. God's telephone lines are always open, and He is waiting to hear from you. He already knows what you are about to say even before you open your mouth.

Instead of complaining and nagging, you can pray. Instead of worrying and fretting, you can pray. In the good times and the bad times, you can pray. But when you pray, don't just tell God what you need from Him. Sit and listen to hear what He needs from you. Be intentional about spending time with Him, whispering prayers throughout the day, and allowing Him to fill you up as you pour yourself out for His glory.

If you ever find yourself trapped in a routine of shallow prayers here are a few suggestions of things you can talk to God about. Pray for your future husband—for God to keep him strong against temptation, for him to walk in his purpose, and for him to be protected from the diabolic plans of the Enemy. Pray for your future children—that God would grant them good health and that they would receive salvation at an early age.

Don't get so caught up in praying for your personal needs and wants in the future that you forget to intercede on behalf of those who need to experience God in the present. Remember to pray for countries suffering from natural disasters, terrorism and wars, for the strength of your pastors, for the protection of your family, for the salvation of your friends, for the healing of your neighbor, for Godly leaders in government, for the unity of the church, for missionaries in foreign lands, for the forgiveness of sins, for orphans, widows and the homeless. Pray for opportunities to serve these people and share the gospel with them. These types of prayers remind you to be sensitive to the burdens of those around you. They help you to remember that life is not just about your comfort and convenience but also meeting the needs of others.

## *Gifted Servant*

Ephesians 2:10 says, "For we are His workmanship, created in Christ Jesus for good works, which God prepared beforehand, that we should walk in them" (ESV). As God's workmanship, you were created on purpose and for a purpose—to complete the good works that you are preordained to do. Every morning when you open your eyes, know there is something that God has prepared for you to do. God gave you unique spiritual gifts that you should be walking in. It is up to you to discover and develop those gifts, and do those good works.

The way to make that discovery is through your involvement. Join a ministry at your church or an extracurricular activity at your school. Mentor a young girl, give back to your community, share your passions, or become a volunteer. Maybe you will discover that your spiritual gift is prophecy, serving, teaching, encouraging, giving, leading, or showing mercy (Romans 12:6-8).
Whatever your gifts are, use them in service to the Lord by serving others. Your gifts are never about self-glorification, but for the edification of those around you. Allow yourself to be a vessel that the Lord uses to make His kingdom come on earth.

Serving others sometimes compel us to 'inconvenience' ourselves for the advancement of God's kingdom. It requires sacrifice and selflessness in going the extra mile to help someone else.

It may mean encouraging non-believers at your work place or showing love to those who need it most. It may mean giving the last of your resources or sacrificing your leisurely weekends to invest in the lives of others. That type of selflessness prepares you for the serving ministry of marriage. Let your future husband meet you work field offering your good works unto the Lord. Together, you both will be servants for His kingdom.

## *Submissive*

Submission has become a despised word for the 21$^{st}$-century woman. We have erroneously associated submission with weakness. We are afraid of losing ourselves in the process of serving someone else. But submission is not about dictatorship but leadership. God has made the husband the head of the wife just as Christ is the head of the church (Ephesians 5:23). Wives are instructed to submit to their husbands in the same way that they submit to the Lord (Ephesians 5:22). Perhaps, that is the real issue. Maybe we have not completely submitted to the Lord and His will, and therefore wrestle with the idea of submitting to a husband.

Maybe we are afraid that the instructions are one-sided. But Ephesians 5:25 goes on to say "Husbands, love your wives, just as Christ loved the church and gave himself up for her" (NIV). The leadership role of the husband requires a sacrificial love. He ought to love his wife the way that he loves his own body (Ephesians 5:28). In the same way that he takes cares of his body, he ought to take care of his wife.

Submission, therefore, does not give the husband permission to be inconsiderate or overly demanding. It does not mean that the husband can treat his wife as his inferior. It also does not mean that the wife should forfeit her contributions and suggestions. Submission certainly does not require the wife to surrender to abuse or anything that goes against the will of God in order to appease her husband.

There will be times of disagreement but submission is the graceful yielding unto the decisions of the husband knowing that he is responsible and answerable to God. It is encouraging and supporting him in his role as the head and your covering. It is using the strength of humility to yield to Godly leadership. This is why it is important for you to wait on the Lord to present you to a Godly man who is first submitted to Him. The last thing you would want is to submit to an ungodly man. Once you have completely submitted to God, you will find it easier to obey His instruction to submit to your future husband.

## *Stewardship*

Stewardship is your ability to responsibly care for the things that God has blessed you with. It means being a servant who is faithful over a few things and can be trusted to rule over many things (Matthew 25:23). Can the Lord trust you to use your time and resources wisely and multiply them for a greater good? Do you maximize the 24-hour loan granted to you each morning? Can He trust you to be a good steward of your financial earnings? What are your current spending habits like? Do you stick to your budget and tithe? Do you take care of your car and house? Do you procrastinate or are you disciplined in working in the spirit of excellence?

I hope the answer to those questions were affirmative. There are probably some areas that can still use some work, and that's okay. Now is the time to begin taking care of what God has blessed you with. Find ways to be faithful in taking care of the little that you have and be content with it. Work diligently toward getting what you really want. Someday you will become an industrious and resourceful wife who knows how to get a bang for her buck.

These are only some of the qualities that are characteristic of a Godly wife. Other qualities like service, forgiveness, respect, and wisdom have already been mentioned throughout the book thus far. All of these fruits come from the root of your relationship with God. The deeper your roots grow in Him, the more you will begin to bear His image in your personal life. Continue to prepare yourself to be your future husband's "good thing." When he finds you, he will not find a girlfriend, but a woman who possesses the qualities of a wife. You've got to be wife material.

## Prayer

Father, I need Your help with cultivating the qualities of a wife. Please teach me how to communicate effectively by being quick to listen and slow to respond. Remind me that the most important conversations of each day are the ones that I have with You. Help me to not be selfish in my prayer requests but to remember the needs of others as well. Heavenly Father, please open my eyes to the works that You have prepared for me to walk in. Help me to discover new ways to serve You by serving others. Jesus, one of the ways that I serve You is by submitting to You. I need you to show me the areas in my life that still need to be completely surrendered. It is only through submitting to You that I can fully submit to my future husband. Finally, I ask that You please help me to take care of the blessings that You have given me and to be content with what I have. Continue to cultivate the qualities of a wife within me so that I can be a good thing to my future husband. Amen.

# CHAPTER TWENTY-THREE

## *A Woman with Goals*

"May He give you the desire of your heart and make all your plans succeed." Psalm 20:4 (NIV)

What have you always wanted to do but have not gotten around to yet? Starting a new business? Writing a song? Volunteering for a worthy cause? Taking online classes? Getting certified in something? Learning a new language or an instrument? What is your goal and how are your working toward achieving it?

Doubt and procrastination are the two things that suffocate goals more than failure does. Doubt will dictate what you cannot do and procrastination will keep you from doing what you can. The only way to uproot doubt is to plant truth. The only way to overcome procrastination is to start in eager anticipation. The achievement of your goals depends on your appetite for success. If you are hungry enough to do something, you will find a way to get it done. Ask yourself "What am I willing to sacrifice to succeed?"

If perfection determines when you will start to work on accomplishing your goals, you will never begin. The "perfect time" will never come; you've got to make the timing perfect. Seize each day and make the most out of the present moment. Just get started! Make a business plan or write a grant proposal. Network with the professionals in the industry you are trying to get into. Improvise and be innovative. Turn your ideas into wise investments. Search for the scholarship. Apply for the internships. Get the expertise and experience you need to go to the next level.

Don't be afraid to take calculated risks. You may not get it right the first time. Maybe you will fail a few times before actually figuring things out. And that's okay. Mistakes are evidence that you are at least trying. You have the choice to either make an effort or an excuse. Don't let the fear of failure stop you from even trying.

If God has given you a vision of what He wants you to do, He will make the provisions. He'll place people in your path to be a blessing, open doors that were closed, and teach you along the way. Your job is to be obedient in taking the first step of faith and trust that He will provide and guide. "Trust in the Lord with all your heart and lean not on your own understanding; in all your ways submit to him, and he will make your paths straight" Proverbs 3: 5–6 (NIV).

Now is the opportune time for you to begin working on your personal, academic, professional, and spiritual goals. Maybe you want to work on eating healthier, improving your grades, start a new job,

## A Woman with Goals

or spend more time in prayer. Maybe you want to try a new activity and develop a new hobby. Whatever the goal is that you want to accomplish, write it down and take manageable steps toward it. Some goals may take two months to accomplish and others may take two years. But no matter how long it takes, do not give up. There may be obstacles along the way but don't quit. You may get frustrated with the process but keep pushing. When things don't go as planned, don't change the goal just change the method you were using to accomplish the goal. Stay positive and remain motivated!

One of the things that I do to keep myself motivated in accomplishing my goals is to create a vision board. On that board are sticky notes, pictures, lists, and reminders of tasks I need to accomplish, long-term resolutions, people I need to reach out to, ways I will get involved, encouraging quotes, and scriptures. I started doing this in college and continued into university. The backdrop of my desks was decorated with scriptures and pictures that kept me encouraged when I felt like the load was too much to carry. I needed something to remind me why I had started my journey and why I needed to finish strong.

In the last semester of graduate school, I remember feeling overwhelmed with assignments. On top of having about six papers to write, my cell phone and computer malfunctioned and I thought I was about to lose my mind. I cried in frustration and literally told God that if He didn't help me, I would not make it through. Sometimes that was the only prayer that I had words to pray. After crying and pouring out my heart to God, I had to dry those tears and get back to work. I took breaks, naps, and trips to the gym in between doing school work in order to cater to my whole being. I called home to get motivation from my family, journaled about how much I needed the Lord, and sang worship songs as I worked into the wee hours of the morning. I sacrificed weekends for studying and catching up on sleep.

For about a month prior to my big day, I hung my dress along with my cap and gown at the very front of my closet as a reminder that the finish line was in sight. Everything that I endured was to get to the finish line of my graduation day and it was worth it! I set a goal to finish graduate school and with the help of the Lord, I did it—one step at a time and one day at a time.

I want to challenge you today to make a list of the goals that you want to accomplish, particularly as a single woman. A few suggestions that you may want to consider are learning how to cook healthy meals, reading more books, getting out of debt, travelling, buying your first car or house, taking a dance class, or learning how to swim. Keep the list of your goals in a place where you will always see them along with a well-developed plan for accomplishing them. Do something every day toward reaching those goals—even if only making a phone call, doing an internet search, or making an appointment.

Remain constructively occupied with your self-development during your single season. Do it for yourself; for your own happiness. Focus on becoming the best version of yourself possible and let your future husband meet you working to achieve your goals. Enter marriage having something to show for the ways you have developed. Don't wait until you are a wife to get to work. Take advantage of the flexibility and freedoms that you have a single woman and maximize this season of your life. It is never too late to begin working toward accomplishing your goals and to dream new dreams. Don't let procrastination and doubt stop you from achieving your goals.

## Prayer

Lord, I pray that my goals and desires will conform to Your will for my life. Thank You for making provisions for my vision. Help me not to procrastinate, but to work diligently toward my goals. Please forgive me for making excuses and being complacent in doing what You have called me to do. Forgive me for trying to accomplish my dreams in my own understanding and strength. Father, I need You to direct my path as I maximize this season of life to develop myself for Your glory. Thank You for not giving up on me and always seeing the best in me. Amen.

# CHAPTER TWENTY-FOUR

## *Virtuous Woman*

"Who can find a virtuous woman? for her price is far above rubies."
Proverbs 31:10 (KJV)

We live in a time when the moral decomposition of society has become more glamorized, televised, and normalized. The world is being driven by pride, flesh, greed, lust, and lawlessness. The grievous fact is that these things are not new under the sun; they are now more ubiquitous because of the media. Immoral activities that were once done privately are now glorified publicly and more often. There are not enough examples of what is means to be a virtuous woman on television, in magazines, on social media, nor in music. Instead, what we see more often are good girls going bad, more women living promiscuous lifestyles, and more women quarrelling and fighting one episode after episode on 'reality' television. What we hear more often are degrading lyrics about women, the objectification of their bodies, and the glorification of premarital sex.

# Virtuous Woman

The accumulation of sparsely clothed women in music videos has sadly become a symbol of success. False conceptions of the value of a woman are perpetuated for the capitalistic purposes of the media.

In a world that celebrates vanity more than virtue, promiscuity more than purity, materials more than morality, and raunchiness more than righteousness, our lives as virtuous women should serve as billboards that seek to change the societal image of women as we bear the image of God.

To examine what it means to be a virtuous woman, let's visit Proverbs 31 for a list of qualities.

> She a precious treasure.
> She is dependable and treats her husband well.
> She dresses well and carries herself with poise.
> She does what she can to provide and prepares meals.
> She awakes before dawn to take care of her family.
> She knows how to become the owner of property.
> She is a diligent worker and is not lazy.
> She helps the poor and the needy.
> Her children are well clothed.
> She is strong, graceful, and excited about her future.
> She speaks words of wisdom and gives thoughtful advice.
> She is worthy of praise for all that she does.

After reading this list and reading the scripture, you may have thought to yourself "gosh, I've got some work to do." Those were my initial sentiments too! I don't know how to make my own garments and I don't prefer to wake up before dawn if I don't have to.

The scripture outlines the virtues of a well-rounded woman who is a good wife and mother, resourceful, meets the needs of herself and others, and shares her wisdom. But the qualities of a Proverbs 31 woman are principles to live by not just a checklist of mundane practices. You may not look for wool and flax to make garments (v.13) and you may not be planting a vineyard (v.16), but that doesn't mean that you are not a virtuous woman. The way that you express your qualities of virtue may be different.

You may not operate a soup kitchen from your house, but you may buy your next door neighbor some groceries. You may not facilitate a mentorship program, but you may give advice to a friend in need. That is the principle of virtuous living—conducting yourself in a moral and Godly manner for His glory. Maybe you possess other virtues that weren't mentioned in Proverbs 31. Those virtues may include dependability, humility, honesty, prudence, purity, modesty, responsibility, patience, charity, dignity, loyalty, and love. Although this is not an exhaustive list of all virtues, possessing any combination of them is praiseworthy.

Even more important than striving to be virtuous like the woman in Proverbs 31, is striving to be like Jesus. Throughout scripture, we see that Jesus is the paragon of virtue. He displayed humility when He took on the form of a human, service when He performed miracles, tact when He dismissed the temptations of Satan on the mountain top, tranquility when He slept on a boat amid the storm, wisdom when He taught in the temples, forbearance when He was whipped and bruised, and love when He died on the cross. As we seek to be more like Jesus, we will begin to bear His image and embody the same virtues that He epitomized.

The personification of Christ-like (virtuous) qualities requires consistent effort, guided thoughts, conscious choices, a supportive community, and the power of the Holy Spirit in order to be developed in us. These virtues in a woman can help to raise generations of Godly children, change misconceptions in our society about the value of women, impact industries for the glory of God, inspire other women to live holy lives, and potentially influence the world as she reflects the image of Christ.

Bearing the image of God means that every day we seek to look more like Him—not just internally but externally as well. Our external appearances open the door for the discussion on the virtue of modesty. When the topic of modesty surfaces in conversation, it often starts with the dire need for men to exercise self-discipline and not feel entitled to the bodies of women—not lusting after them, inappropriately touching them, or making lewd comments regardless of the way they are dressed. That is absolutely true!

The conversation may then carry on with the mentioning of women not leading their brothers to sin by putting a stumbling block in their way (Romans 14:13). That is also not only true, but biblical. This is the part of the conversation where a comment like "I should be able to wear whatever I want" comes in, along with a dissention in dispositions. But instead of debating dress codes down to inches and centimeters, I want to help you to understand that the foundation of modesty transcends the covering of the body. Modesty has more to do with the condition of the heart and the handling beauty rather than the hiding of it.

Modesty is the presenting and deporting of ourselves in a manner that reflects the dignity and value that God has created us with. If a virtuous woman is more precious than rubies, then someone that is precious ought to be protected—having respectful privacy of the body. Women choose their clothing based on many factors from comfort, to functionality, to occasion, to weather, to individuality, and personality. Our bodies vary in shapes and sizes and clothing for various body types should be taken into consideration as well. There is nothing wrong with wanting to feel beautiful in an outfit, embracing our femininity, and loving our bodies. To make a legalistic guideline of how long and loose our clothing should be will only complicate the discussion unnecessarily. The bottom line is that the way we dress reflects the way we view ourselves internally.

Whether dressed in oversized clothing because of an insecurity or revealingly to seek the wrong type of attention, those are issues of the heart. The world doesn't have to see all our skin in order to prove that we are comfortable in it. Whether men lust after women in a potato sack or women wearing skin-tight clothing, is also an issue of lust in the heart. So let's get to the *heart* of the matter.

If the way that we dress is a reflection of the way that we view ourselves, then modesty requires us to view ourselves through the lens of God. Since He created us with dignity and great value, the first question that we should ask ourselves when getting dressed is "Does this outfit reflect my God-given dignity and does it respectfully preserves the private regions of my body?" Secondly, if everything we do ought to honor God, the next question we should ask is "Are my intentions for wearing this outfit pure and does it reflect the image of God?" Thirdly, we should ask ourselves "Is what I am wearing appropriate for the occasion?" We wouldn't wear a swimsuit at work, a raincoat on a sunny day, or flip flops during the winter simply because it is inappropriate. If the answers to these three questions are affirmative, the virtue of modestly is most likely being displayed. If you are still uncertain, here's a final question to ask yourself. "Would I be ashamed or feel uncomfortable in these clothes if I were to meet Jesus today?

When we begin to see ourselves the way that God sees us, it is through those same lenses that we will begin to see the dignity and value in others as well. Only then can we bring an end to the objectification of women, the exploitation of their bodies, inappropriate touching and remarks, and the erroneous association of their value with their bodies.

The virtue of modesty is so much more than the clothing we wear. So much more than following rules about what not to wear. It is about the lifestyle we live. Everything we do, including the way we that dress should point people back to God and not draw attention to ourselves out of vainglory or conceit. When our hearts are humbled, we are able to hear when God tells us about our clothing, receive conviction from the Holy Spirit, and listen to the advice of a friend or trusted voice concerning our clothing.

Modesty should not be legalistic, but rather a choice to trust that God is protecting and not restraining us. He wants us to firstly clothe our hearts with dignity and respect. The Lord is more interested in a change in heart, not just a change in clothing.

Virtuous women are not rarities. There are not enough of them portrayed in the media but certainly, there are many women who are striving to be Christ-like. Although it is not easy, remember that you are an image bearer of God. Don't allow the pressure of this world to make you feel inferior for having morals, good character, virtues, and taking a stand for righteousness. Be the salt in bland places and light in dark places. Run your beautiful feet to proclaim the good news (Isaiah 52:7) that it is meritorious to be virtuous.

## Prayer

Lord, I want to be a well-rounded woman who takes care of myself, my family and those around me. Help me to develop the principles of a Proverbs 31 woman as I seek to be more like You. Even though this world is filled with vanity, pride, lawlessness, greed, and lust, I want to bear Your image. Give me the courage to display honorable and praiseworthy qualities in an immoral world. Let others see You through me—in the way that I speak, dress, and live. Amen.

# CHAPTER TWENTY-FIVE

## *What's the Motive?*

"Test me, LORD, and try me, examine my heart and my mind."
Psalm 26:2 (NIV)

When I was a little girl I would always accompany my mom to the grocery store on Saturday mornings. She sometimes sent me on escapades to weigh fruits and pick up vegetables. I learned how to examine produce for their freshness and quality. Sometimes my mom made jokes about how the limes that I chose were so hard that they could give her arthritis. It was an honor to have the responsibility of picking the bunch of bananas that were neither extremely ripe nor extremely green. I took pride in bagging the tomatoes that didn't have bruises or blemishes and presenting them to my mom for her approval. But on my way to the produce department, I would always be captivated by the wall of toy vending machines at the front of the store. My eyes would be fixated on the machines with the plastic spherical containers holding neatly folded five-dollar bills along with some other uninteresting toys. After inserting a quarter into the machine, each time I would twist the knob and hope that the containers with money would be dispensed. To my dismay, the money containers always seemed to be at the top of the pile in the machine. I would always end up settling for the stickers or some other toy and walk out of the store in disappointment.

In my naïve mind, I thought that I could twist the knob to manipulate the machine to dispense the containers that I really wanted. Suffice it to say that I never won because I have learned that twisting the knob did not manipulate the machine into getting what I wanted.

Let's be honest. Sometimes as single women we treat our relationship with God just like that toy vending machine. We put in *quarters* of Bible study, church attendance, sexual purity, and ministry with the expectation of getting a husband as a 'prize.' But a relationship with God is not like turning the knob on a vending machine. God cannot be manipulated and we can never twist His arm to make Him give us what we want. He doesn't owe us a reward every time that we go to church or give an offering. It is by His love and grace that He dispenses His blessings upon us—not because we can do acts of righteousness to earn or deserve them.

Ask yourself about your motive for serving God. Is it because you want money or a new car in return? Is it because you want to finally be married? There is nothing wrong with inherently desiring these kinds of blessings but they cannot be the motivation for serving God. Any motivation for worshiping God that is external to the fact

## What's the Motive?

that He is worthy—whether He gives us blessings or not—is feeble and insufficient to keep our hearts engaged in service. If marriage or any other blessing are the only motivations for serving God, then as soon as we get what we want, our worship will cease.

When we serve God with ulterior motives, everything we do from prayer to praise will begin to feel dull and dispirited—the same way I felt every time that I walked out of the grocery store without the prize that I really wanted. We should not just come to God bringing sacrifices of good works as 'quarters' only when we want something from Him. He is not a Jack-in-the-Box toy that can be wound up at our convenience to oblige our requests because He is not obligated to do so.

Our worship should spring from a heart of love and gratitude for who God is, not just for what He can give. If we base our love for God on what He gives to us, we would have a skewed view of Him because He doesn't always give us what we want. Sometimes the things that we want may not be good for us during a particular season of our lives. It is because of God's love for us that He doesn't always grant us what we want, but He always gives us what we need.

God doesn't cease to be good when we don't get what we want. He sees the desires of our hearts and wants them to be surrendered to Him. Those desires for something or someone should not overpower our desire for Him. Matthew 6:33 tells us that our first motive should be to seek the kingdom of God and His righteousness. Then everything else, including marriage, will be added if it is in His will.

Always remember that marriage is not the ultimate end goal of life, the solution to all our problems, nor the means to complete happiness (read that again). It is an inadequate space-filler for the heart that has the wrong view of the desires that it pursues. In our hearts, our desire for God must be stronger than our desire for marriage or anything else.

With this understanding, I ask, can you still serve God with a cheerful spirit even if it means waiting a little longer before He reveals you to your future husband? Will you continue to be faithful to Him? Can you trust Him to fulfill the desires of your heart in His timing? I hope that you can because marriage not the purpose of serving God. It is merely an opportunity for you to model His relationship with the church.

In my personal life, I constantly pause for what I call "heart checks" to be certain that my motives are pure and that my heart is in the right posture. I would ask the Lord to search my heart and to remove anything that hinders me from serving Him with sincere and selfless motivations. My ways may seem pure in my own eyes but God weighs my motives (Proverbs 16:2)..

We may be able to deceive ourselves but we can never deceive God. So be honest. Be real in recognizing the ways that you have tried to selfishly manipulate God in order to get what you want. Ask for His forgiveness for the times that you were more occupied with your own desires than pursuing His purposes. Let us strive to purify our motives by asking God for a heart that has the right view of Him. A view that acknowledges that His goodness is not contingent on whether He grants our desires. He is good and worthy to be praised regardless.

I encourage you to conduct your own heart checks and to examine your motives for everything that you do—from the way that you interact with people, to the photos that you post on social media. Ask yourself difficult questions. "Am I being flirtatious because I want attention or am I being genuinely friendly?" "Am I posting because I know something that people need to hear or because I have the *need* to be heard?" "Am I trying to draw attention to God or to myself?"

If the motives are selfish then the actions should be suspended because when our motives aren't right, then our messages may be wrong. Make it a habit to stop and think about whether the things we say and do are inspiring, necessary, and helpful. Let's begin checking our hearts before checking in on Facebook. Let's check our motives before posting our moves on Instagram. Most of all, let us not get so caught up in our desires for earthly blessings that we forget to be eternally-minded.

## Prayer

Search me, Lord and all my motives. If there is anything that does not look like You, please purge me of it. Please forgive me for the times that I have served You with selfish motivations. You are worthy of my praise regardless of whether You lift another finger to give me something. Wash me and purify my heart. May the words of my mouth and the meditation of my heart be acceptable in Your sight. Amen.

# CHAPTER TWENTY-SIX

## *Red Flags*

"Be on guard. Stand firm in the faith. Be courageous. Be strong." 1 Corinthians 16:13 (NLT)

"Stay alert! Watch out for your great enemy, the devil. He prowls around like a roaring lion, looking for someone to devour." 1 Peter 5:8 (NLT)

If you are remotely interested in American football, you may be familiar with the term "flag on the field." If the coach of a team wants to challenge a call made by the referee, a red flag can be thrown onto the field to indicate the challenge. A specific play is brought under revision before progressing in the game. Red flags in a relationship work the same way. When you identify something that makes you uncomfortable you can throw the red flag on the field and challenge those words, behaviors, or patterns. They should never be ignored but observed and investigated when necessary. Ask the difficult questions, have tough conversations, and find the underlying cause of the matter at hand.

Many women who have ignored the red flags while dating later end up wishing that they were more vigilant, paid closer attention, listened to their intuition, and dug a little bit deeper. Does that mean you need to behave like an FBI agent for every little hiccup in a relationship? No! You don't have to be mistrustful about everything but at least be mindful. Be present. Be alert. Don't get so caught up in your feelings that you allow emotions to overpower reason and passion to override prudence.

Whenever we don't recognize red flags and call them as they are, the signs that indicate danger tend to become distorted as something trivial. We start to make excuses and find false security by ignoring the warning signs. When driving a car and the light for low fuel level comes on, we immediately find the nearest gas station for refueling. It is evident that we can only go so far before the car is devoid of fuel and is unable to keep going. So why do we continue to ignore the indicators in relationships? Why do we drive past the red flags?

Distortions of the truth are deceitful to our realities. These distortions result in the behaviors that need to be corrected, never being confronted. It is then that sympathy overrides common sense, obsession is mistaken for admiration, possessiveness is confused with protectiveness, insecurities are passed off as confidence, and jealousy is disguised as concern. Sometimes we don't pick up that we are being manipulated and exploited because we're too deep in our emotions.

Preferences become demands, wants become needs, concern becomes control, exclusivity becomes ownership, choices turn into ultimatums, and sweet talk turns into bitter lies.

I want to help you keep your eyes and ears opened for red flags within your relationship with a man who may be a potential love interest. Below is a list of signs that indicate the need for you to throw your flag on the field. They may show that the person you are dealing with is not your future husband.

- ***He is not an active Christian.***

This is number one on this list for a reason. You cannot go a step further with any man who is not pursuing Christ. It is one thing to receive salvation and another to live a life of consecration. Be careful to not 'fall' for a man who may be saved but is not actively seeking the things of Christ. He should do more than attend church or recite scriptures. Any man can go to church and repeat scriptures that have never taken root in his heart or transformed his life. There is absolutely no compromising on this one because you'd otherwise be starting the relationship being unequally yoked.

- ***He speaks or treats you in a disrespectful manner.***

If a man intentionally tells you things to make you feel slighted or to degrade you, then he reveals insecurity within himself. If the relationship starts off with disrespect, then the frequency of his negative behavior may escalate from rare occasions to common occurrences. Pay attention to the way he treats other women in his life like his mother, aunts, or sisters. His behavior toward them is a great sign of how he will treat you.

- ***He practices infidelity.***

If he cannot be faithful to you now, do you think he will ever be faithful when you get married? Don't fool yourself into believing that marriage can change a man—only God can. It doesn't matter how beautiful you are and how well you can cook, a person who is not ready to commit will not be able to complement you in marriage. Respect yourself enough to not be treated as an option when you deserve to be a priority.

- ***He has no ambition or goals that he is working toward.***

If he cannot tell you where he sees himself in the next five years and what he hopes to have accomplished, you are looking at potentially dragging around dead weight. You need someone who can complement the goals that you are already working toward, not detract from them. It is one thing to have grandiose ideas and plans and another to w diligently work toward them.

- ***He intentionally breaches boundaries that you have asked him not to cross.***

If you told him not to touch you in a certain way, to not call you after a certain time, or not to cross certain conversational lines, and he still does, this is a sign that he does not respect your personal boundaries.

- ***He is controlling and overbearing.***

If he needs to know where you are, what you are doing, and who you are with every single minute of the day, you may have a serious case of insecurity on your hands. A man who is controlling is also likely to be abusive. Beware!

- ***He has a problem managing his anger.***

If his temper flares up easily, he makes an argument out of the simplest things, or he expresses violent tantrums, then this may be a sign of anger management issues. These warning signs should not be ignored as they too can also be telltale signs of abuse. A man that has an easily flared temper can likely explode on you. Your niceness to him may prove to be futile and exhausting if the source of his anger is not completely resolved with the help of the Lord.

- **He gives you the silent treatment.**

If he stops talking to you without an explanation and ignores your calls you may need to take this as an indicator and keep it moving. He's probably not wholeheartedly interested in you or is not ready to commit.

- **He doesn't tell the truth.**

If every word that comes out of his mouth is a lie, and you don't even know when to believe him, you are setting yourself up for unnecessary stress and games that you don't have time to play.

- **He is manipulative.**

If he tries to twist things around to get his way, you may have a problem on your hands. If he preys on your emotional vulnerabilities and gentleness to impose his own agenda, be wary. He may even propose ultimatums and make threats in order to control you. If you notice any of these behaviors, you are in an unhealthy situation and you should leave before his manipulation becomes a trap of bondage and abuse.

- **He doesn't take responsibility for his actions.**

If he always plays the blame game and can never take responsibility, you may be dealing with a child in a man's body. A man should be teachable and willing to admit when he is wrong. He should take the necessary actions to correct himself.

- **He tells you what you need to do to look "better."**

This is a major one! The second you hear the words "If only...," your ears should become more alert. If he tells you that you should lose weight, bleach your skin, wear weave, or do anything else just to be beautiful in his eyes, there is a problem. No one should require you to make major changes to yourself just so you can be more attractive to them. Sister, he can take you or leave you, just as you are! Any changes that you make, do it for your own sake and on your own volition not because you are being pressured to appease someone else's desires.

- **He is self-centered.**

Be careful of any man that doesn't care about anyone or anything besides himself. Maybe he dominates conversations, only wants to do the activities that are of interest to him, or never asks how you are doing. If his world revolves around himself and he has no regard for the concerns of others, then there may not be any space for you and the things of concern to you.

- **He bears it all too soon.**

Be wary of a guy who tells you that he loves you within three weeks of meeting him. That may sound funny but I'm serious. You have not had enough time to build a steady foundation. This can be a sign that he is obsessing over you and probably have some insecurity issues. These men may be seeking your validation and a stroke to their ego, particularly if they are rebounding from a previous relationship. This premature confession of 'love' pressures you to reciprocate those feelings when you haven't even decided if you like him—his character and qualities. Don't force yourself to make anyone 'the one' just because they wore their hearts on their sleeves very early on. Don't confuse infatuation with true love.

- **He tries to move too quickly.**

What's the rush? The best of relationships is built on the foundation of friendship. But if you speed past the friendship stage, you will deprive yourself of the opportunity to learn more about the person—their history, interests, habits, and aspirations—and settle into a relationship with someone you know nothing about. A man who tries to push things too quickly usually has an agenda but you won't be able to discern it by rushing the relationship.

When we move too quickly, we inhibit the keenness of our discernment, our ability to notice red flags and to ask the right questions. Do not allow men to play in the sandbox of our heart as if your emotions were toys. Slow down! Anything worth having takes time.

- **He is behaving secretively.**

A man who is being secretive often has a secret. If he has to hide his phone every time it rings, or remove himself from your presence to answer phone calls, something is definitely abnormal. If he starts to get overly defensive for the simplest of questions, something is not right. Now before you go off into FBI mode, I'm not telling you to demand his passwords and become a nag. I'm also not telling you to be overly suspicious and insecure about his every move. Use wisdom and discernment, and pay attention to whether these behaviors become a pattern. Then you can proceed prayerfully.

- **There is disagreement with your core values.**

Only you know what your core values are. They may include your relationship with God, connectedness to family, healthy diet, loyalty, honesty, and adventure. These values are central to the way you live your life and may even serve as guiding principles. If you and your person of interest do not agree completely on these core values, there will inevitably be a clash. The differences in the values that drive you both may end up driving you apart. The two of you cannot move forward unless you are moving in the same direction. You both need to be on the same track and on the same train.

- **He is still hung up on past relationships.**

If your person of interest always brings up ex-girlfriends or failed marriages, it is a good sign that he has not yet moved on from those relationships. Maybe there are still open wounds that need to be stitched and healed before he can ever be completely emotionally available to you. The last thing you want is to be compared to another woman. There should not be competition between you and anyone from his past. You may need to give him some space to figure out what he really wants and drop the baggage he is still carrying.

- **He tries to keep you away from your family or spiritual mentors.**

This is a huge red flag! Your family and spiritual mentors serve as your covering and they have your best interest at heart. If your partner does not want to be introduced to those people or tries to keep you away from them, then he is probably not willing to have accountability or glean from the wisdom they have to offer in the relationship.

- *He is emotionally unstable.*

If you don't know what kind of person you will be dealing with on any given day or his mood suddenly changes from one extreme to the next, you may want to take the high road. It is difficult to build a healthy relationship with this type of person.

- *No one else knows that you are in a relationship.*

To this point, I have one thing to say. If he cannot claim you in public, then he shouldn't keep you in private.

- *He needs you to constantly validate him.*

If you have to keep telling a man that he is handsome and reassure him that you do love and care about him, he may have insecurity issues. While compliments are lovely from time to time, if you constantly have to reassure him of his value just to boost his ego, this is a major red flag. If he doesn't see himself as being valuable because he was created in the image of God, you can complement him 100 times in a day and he will still feel unworthy. That is an internal insecurity that he needs God's help to correct.

- *His friends display behaviors that are unacceptable to you.*

I'm sure you have heard the adage "birds of a feather flock together." If his friends display behaviors that are unacceptable to you, more than likely your person of interest is the exact same way. His friends can give you a good indication of who he is.

These are only some of red flags that you need to pay attention to. If I were to mention them all, this would be an exhaustive list. I encourage you to use wisdom and discernment, particularly at the beginning stages of any friendship or relationship to identify these and other red flags. Look out for consistency in what the person says and does. Listen to the content of the conversations. Pay keen attention to deal-breakers (non-negotiable qualities) in your love interest that nullify the possibility of being in a committed relationship with them. Ask for the advice of a mature and trusted person or couple who may be able to see what you cannot. Finally, pray about all of your relationships. Spiritually discern the people you are connecting yourself with, giving your heart to, and spending your time with.

Be sensitive to the voice and direction of the Holy Spirit when He tells you to withdraw or to engage. When He shows you, or tells you something, do not avoid it but rather address it promptly and appropriately. Red flags are red for a reason. They are like traffic lights that signal you to stop and evaluate a situation before moving ahead.

Sometimes we tend to operate solely in the emotions of our hearts and not the wisdom of our heads. We wrestle to keep people in our lives that God is trying to get us to let go of. Without the guidance of the Holy Spirit, we will find ourselves being deceived, disappointed, broken-hearted, and regretful. I pray that we will be obedient to God's instructions without hesitation.

There is no need to get 'super spiritual' about situations that God has already given us clear and simple answers to. We sometimes pray the same prayers over and over and ask God for signs, wonders, prophecies, and miracles when He has already told us how to handle a situation. When you notice red flags that are destructive and God is instructing you to walk away, do not cling to that person for your own selfish reasons. Instead, pray for the will of God, and believe that His plans are perfect. Trust that even if you don't understand, that His plan for your life is good.

## Prayer

Father, please give me Your wisdom and open my eyes to things I might normally overlook. I ask for the leading of Your Holy Spirit and guidance in my relationships. Give me the courage to confront red flags and to be obedient when you tell me to walk away. Help me to stand firmly in obedience to Your instructions and to not make excuses to hold on to my personal will. I believe that Your plan for my life is perfect and I trust Your voice. Amen.

# CHAPTER TWENTY-SEVEN

## *Hold Out for Your Husband*

"To everything there is a season, and a time to every purpose under the heaven." Ecclesiastes 3:1 (NIV)

The greatest gift you can give to God is your entire life. The greatest gift you can give to yourself is becoming whole. And the greatest gift you can give to your future husband is to be a wife who is ready to walk with him to fulfill a divine purpose under heaven. Your journey to wholeness during your singleness will usher you into your season of being a helpmeet. And although your season of singleness may not prepare you for every aspect of marriage, your wholeness in Christ will be everything you need to thrive. Allow the Lord to take you through the process of letting go of your past, finding contentment in your present, and preparing you for your future as a Godly wife. He will empower you to be strong against the pressures of society and to uphold a standard of holiness and purity. Always remember that you are a gift to your future husband. Become the best version of yourself so that you can add value to his life.

Singleness is not a disease, a state of being, or an identity. It is merely a temporary season of your life that will come and go just like the autumn, winter, spring, and summer. Every season in life is beautiful and it is up to you to find the blessing and beauty in it. Don't spend so much time thinking about the destination of a relationship that you do not enjoy the journey of preparation to getting there. Everything is beautiful in God's time.

There will be times when you get tired of waiting but remember that there is no waste in waiting on God's timing. In those moments, pour your heart out before God in worship and spend some intimate time in His presence. Every day we must continue trusting, continue waiting, continue growing, and continue going.

Choose to be happy. Choose to enjoy the present moment. Choose to not settle for less than you deserve. Choose to wait on God's choice and allow Him to write your love story. Choose to be content while yielding your desires to the Lord. Choose to have the right view of God—He is good and everything that He does is good. Choose to spend your time and resources for the glory of God. Choose to desire God more than you desire anyone or anything else. Choose to bear His image. Most of all, choose to pursue Him, to pursue your purpose, and to live your life to the fullest right now.

Here are my final words of encouragement for wherever you may find yourself on your journey to wholeness.

To the single woman who feels overlooked, know that you are precious in the eyes of God. He sees you, loves you, and values you. To the woman who is looking for 'the one,' focus more on being the one. You don't have to look because you will be found and presented to your future husband. To the woman who is a serial dater, remember that relationships will become feeble space-fillers if your heart doesn't first find complete satisfaction in Christ. To the lady with 'the list' there is nothing wrong with knowing which qualities you admire and desire in a man. But do not cling to that list so tightly that you leave no room for God to give you not just what you want but also what you need. Don't be so shallow that you miss a great friendship with a male because you judge him based on his external appearance that doesn't precisely match your 50-item list.

To the lady who is seeking attention on social media, you don't need to post 5,000 revealing photos of yourself to affirm your value. Your value does not come from the person who clicks the "like" button but by the person who proved your worth by dying on a cross for you. To the woman whose heart has been broken multiple times, please don't allow your past experiences to cause you to give up on true love. Every man does not have intentions of hurting you. To the woman looking for stability and security in a man, your future husband will be your spouse, not your Savior. Learn to depend on God to provide your needs. To the woman watching her biological clock, the same God that gave Sarah a baby at the age of 90 is the same God that can bless you with a child. To the woman who is crying on the couch, your future husband cannot find you if you stay locked away in the house. You've got to get up and get out. Treat yourself and place yourself in positive communities and events. That doesn't mean that you should go out with the intention to seduce a man, but position yourself to be found.

I don't know when the Lord will present you to your future husband. But I do know that the wait will be worth it. So hold out for your husband.

## Prayer

Lord, I choose to be content during this season of singleness. I surrender my desire for marriage to You. Please teach me the lessons that You need me to learn, mature me in the areas that I am underdeveloped, purge me of my past baggage, and prepare me to be a Godly wife. Thank you for renewing my mindset of what it means to be a wife in waiting and helping me to see my singleness as a beautiful gift. Let my heart find rest in You as I completely surrender all of my anxieties and fears. Lord, I refuse to allow the influences of society to distract me from the work that You are doing in my life. Help me to remain focused on maximizing the purpose for which I was created. Most of all Lord, I want my heart to desire You more than it desires anyone or anything else because it is only in You that I can find wholeness in my singleness. Amen.

# *Bonus*

Whenever you believe you have come across your future husband, there are a lot of questions that you need to ask throughout the relationship. That's what dating is all about—getting the details. Asking questions are the only way to find out whether the man sitting across from you is marriage material. You need to dig deeper than superficial questions about favorite color and food. Get down to the practical details who he really is. Here are a few questions to keep the conversation going. Pay attention to red flags that may arise and call a 'time out' to dig deeper. In no particular order, here are they:

1. What is your real name?
2. Are you biologically male or female?
3. Are you attracted to women, men, or both?
4. Who are you? What is your identity outside of this relationship?
5. Where are you from/where did you grow up?
6. What do your parents do as an occupation?
7. What is their relationship like?
8. Do you have a relationship with your father, and does he play an active role in your life? If not, how has that impacted you?
9. Are you a "mama's boy?"
10. How do you treat your mother and other women?

Bonus

11. What do you value in a woman?
12. Do you believe in gender roles?
13. What do you value about me?
14. Have you prayed about me? What did God say?
15. Can you pray for me? Like right now? ☺
16. What is your view of marriage, and what expectations do you have?
17. Do you have any reservations about this relationship?
18. Are we in a relationship with the purpose of marriage?
19. How much reading or research have you done about having a successful marriage?
20. How have you personally prepared for marriage?
21. What is your biggest fear in a relationship? Are you afraid of commitment?
22. What is your view of courtship versus dating?
23. Are you a family-oriented person? If so, what do you like to do with them?
24. Do you have unresolved family issues?
25. Do you live with your parents or alone?
26. Do you have a child/children? If so, what is your relationship like with the mother(s) of your child/children?
27. Do you want children? How many?
28. What are your views on adoption?
29. What is your idea of a Godly father?
30. What does it mean to be the priest of your home, provider, protector, and nurturer?

31. What do you believe are the best ways to parent a child?
32. What kind of education should children have?
33. Do you believe in disciplining children? How?
34. Have you ever been engaged or married before? If so, what was the cause of your separation or divorce?
35. What are your goals in life?
36. Where do you see yourself five to ten years from now?
37. What do you do in your spare time?
38. Have you ever been incarcerated?
39. Have you ever been involved in a lawsuit?
40. What do you own or want to own for yourself?
41. What are you passionate about?
42. What is your greatest accomplishment thus far?
43. How do you really feel about yourself?
44. How much do you actually know about yourself? What do you still want to learn?
45. What are you commonly misunderstood for?
46. What do you want your life's legacy to be?
47. What are your spending habits like? Do you tithe? Do you save money?
48. Are you in debt?
49. Do you gamble?
50. Did you go to college?
51. What is your occupation?
52. What is your work schedule like?
53. Has your work ever resulted in a breakup?
54. What are your views on… (adoption, abortion, racism etc.)?

Bonus

55. What are your views on infidelity, adultery, fornication, and divorce?
56. What are your views on premarital sex/kissing/other displays of affection?
57. What is the purpose of your life, and why were you created?
58. Do you keep a lot of friends?
59. Are you a wild partier/clubber?
60. Are you an active believer? Are you involved in ministry?
61. What is your relationship like with God?
62. Who is your role model?
63. Do you have a church home?
64. Are you religious or spiritual?
65. Are you a virgin? Are you celibate?
66. What are your most outstanding qualities?
67. Are you a procrastinator?
68. Are you teachable?
69. Are you controlling?
70. How do you make decisions?
71. What grinds your gears?
72. How do you manage conflict?
73. Do you have a criminal record/ have you ever been arrested/in jail?
74. Can you cook and clean?
75. What is your diet like?
76. Are you willing to undergo a physical health exam before marriage?
77. Are you taking any medications?

78. Have you ever had surgeries?

79. Do you have insurance?

80. What is your emotional, mental and physical health like? Do you have chronic or acute diseases?

81. What are you like when you get sick? What do you need?

82. Can you step up if I were to develop an illness?

83. Do you drink or smoke?

84. How have you impacted the lives of others?

85. How do you manage your anger?

86. What do you do when you feel lonely?

87. How do you overcome temptation?

88. Have you ever been abused? How did you deal with that?

89. Are there any voids in your life that have not been filled?

90. Do you have deep and dark secrets? What are they?

91. Do you have trust issues? How could you deal with that?

92. What are you insecure about?

93. What makes you unique?

94. What is your cultural background? How does it now impact your life?

95. Are there any cultural or family traditions customs that you keep?

96. Are you able to show love toward others from a different ethnic, racial, cultural, economic etc. background from you? What are your family's views on these differences?

97. Do you enjoy travelling?

98. How do you practice effective communication?

99. What is your primary love language?

Bonus

100.   What makes you feel happy, afraid, insecure?

## About the Author

Brittney Jones is a young Bahamian author currently residing in Nassau, Bahamas. She enjoys avid journaling and writing poetry. One of her short pieces was published in the Young Writers' *Mini Sagas: Tales From Around the World* book. Brittney desires to challenge single young women to maximize their purpose and to find wholeness in God as they pursue holiness. She wants to use her wisdom to help them confront heart issues in preparation for becoming helpmeets.

## Contact the Author

Email: wholenessinsingleness@gmail.com
Facebook: @brittneyiRepChrist
Instagram: @brittneyirepchrist

# About the Foreword Contributor

Bishop Robert C. Blakes, Jr. is the devote husband of Lisa Blakes and the couple has four biological children. He is the senior pastor of New Home Family Worship Center in New Orleans, Louisiana and Houston, Texas. Bishop Blakes has earned a Master's degree of Theology from Christian Bible College of Louisiana and has been in ministry for over three decades. He is a highly sought after empowerment speaker and a profound teacher of the gospel.

Bishop Blakes is a regular teacher on the Word Harvest International Television, and he co-hosts a weekly television broadcast with his brother Samuel Bakes on the Word Network. He and his family also operate KKNO Christian Radio Station in New Orleans. RC Blakes has impacted thousands of women through the penning of his book *Father Daughter Talk* and ongoing teachings on Periscope.

His teachings offer practical principles from the Word of God to empower, encourage and educate.

## Contact R.C. Blakes

**Website:** www.rcblakes.com
**Youtube:** @Robert Blakes
**Periscope:** @RC_Blakes
**Facebook:** @RCBlakes
**Twitter:** @RC_Blakes
**Instagram:** @rcblakes

Made in the USA
Columbia, SC
16 July 2017